G.O.A.T.

MAKING THE CASE FOR THE GREATEST OF ALL TIME

SERENA
WILLIAMS

BY TAMI CHARLES

STERLING CHILDREN'S BOOKS
New York

STERLING CHILDREN'S BOOKS
New York

An Imprint of Sterling Publishing Co., Inc.
1166 Avenue of the Americas
New York, NY 10036

ISBN 978-1-4549-3201-7

Distributed in Canada by Sterling Publishing Co., Inc.
c/o Canadian Manda Group, 664 Annette Street
Toronto, Ontario M6S 2C8, Canada
Distributed in the United Kingdom by GMC Distribution Services
Castle Place, 166 High Street, Lewes, East Sussex BN7 1XU, England
Distributed in Australia by NewSouth Books
University of New South Wales, Sydney, NSW 2052, Australia

For information about custom editions, special sales, and premium
and corporate purchases, please contact Sterling Special Sales at
800-805-5489 or specialsales@sterlingpublishing.com.

Manufactured in Singapore

Lot #:
2 4 6 8 10 9 7 5 3 1
02/20

sterlingpublishing.com

Cover and interior design by Heather Kelly

Cover and interior image credits are on page 128

CONTENTS

INTRODUCTION: WHAT IS A G.O.A.T?

Acronyms are the coolest, aren't they? In pop culture, we use them all the time to shorten long phrases. BFF (best friends forever), OMG (oh my goodness), and ASAP (as soon as possible) are a few you might have heard. In sports, the most desired acronym of all is G.O.A.T. And no, it doesn't refer to the barnyard animal, cute as it is!

A **G.O.A.T.** is the best, the ultimate, the Greatest of All Time! The G.O.A.T. can be found in many arenas: in the boxing ring, the tennis court, and even in an Olympic pool. One thing is for sure: Becoming the G.O.A.T. isn't easy. Becoming a great athlete takes skill, perseverance, and undeniable talent. But to become not just great, but the greatest *of all time*, well, you need to be all that and even more.

To be fair, calling someone the "greatest" is an opinion. An opinion is a judgment or conviction of something you believe is true. Some G.O.A.T.s are easy to agree on, and others . . . not so much. Opinions vary and, after all, you can measure greatness in different ways. For example, if you ask boxing fans to name the greatest boxer of all time is, Muhammad Ali might be a popular answer. Why? Because he had 37 knockouts, won an **Olympic** gold medal, and was heavyweight champion of the world three times. Not only did he call himself the greatest, he wrote a book about it! But other boxing fans might say that Joe Louis is the greatest of all time. After all, he finished his career with 51 knockouts and held the record of heavyweight champ for 140 consecutive months. If we're looking at knockouts alone, clearly Joe Louis surpasses Muhammad Ali. But is that enough to be the greatest?

Sports fans love to debate who the G.O.A.T. is for their beloved sport. To know the G.O.A.T., you really have to know the sport. But don't worry. Our handy info boxes throughout should keep you up to speed. Fan choices for the G.O.A.T. might be based on a variety of factors: records held, titles earned, or medals won.

The world of tennis is no exception. Tennis fans love to debate who the greatest player of all time might be. So who is it? Who is the G.O.A.T. of tennis? Could it be Roger Federer, who holds the record for the most Grand Slam singles titles in men's tennis, with 20? Others might say that Billie Jean King is the greatest, not because of her Grand Slam singles titles (12, to be exact), but more importantly because of the power of her legacy. Billie proudly fought for women's equality on and off the court and was a pioneer in advocating for female athletes to be paid as well as male athletes. Now *that* is pretty awesome!

All of these tennis players are great athletes, maybe even legends. They have all demonstrated skill, talent, and perseverance in their career. But which of them has that something more, that something special that would truly give them the crown? Because if we're talking G.O.A.T., then there is another player we need to consider. A girl from Compton, California. A player who came from humble beginnings and won 23 Grand Slam singles titles, more than any man or woman. A woman who is still in the game, and is in it to keep winning. You may have heard of her. Her name is Serena Williams.

Is Serena the G.O.A.T.? Let's weigh the evidence and draw a conclusion.

FUN FACT!

Known as the world's greatest sporting contest, the original **Olympic** games were held in Greece over 3,000 years ago. By 1896, the Olympics included 280 "male-only" contestants from 13 nations, competing in 43 sporting events, such as tennis, swimming, and weight lifting. Today's Olympics feature both men and women from hundreds of nations and take place every four years, with summer and winter Olympics alternating every two years.

1992: Serena Williams in action on the tennis court

1

HUMBLE BEGINNINGS

Some stars are made by chance, others by choice. Tennis star Serena Williams was made by a bit of both. On June 11, 1978 Virginia Ruzici won the Women's Final of the French Open. Security guard and divorced father of six, Richard Williams, watched this moment with stars in his eyes. Ruzici's prize money for one day of work was $40,000, which was more than Richard could ever make in a full year.

Growing up in Shreveport, Louisiana, Richard experienced poverty, racism, and violence, particularly when he was attacked as a teen by a group of white peers who demanded that Richard call them "Mister." Beaten and bloodied, he refused. Richard believed that he deserved to be treated fairly, and as an equal. He didn't want his children to have a future where they felt anything less than extraordinary. Even as a teenager, Richard knew he would want to make a better life for his family. Given the hardships he faced in his youth, when he saw Virginia play, Richard began to see tennis as a way for his family to have a better life. Maybe his own children could rule the tennis world like Virginia Ruzici did on that day in June 1978.

In 1979, in Michigan, he met Oracene Price, a nurse and widowed mother of three. Oracene shared his vision of raising daughters who could become champions. Tennis could be a way to open doors for their children, even though participating in the sport came with a long list of challenges. Tennis wasn't just a sport that you picked up like a hobby. You had to be *born* into the game. Play the game long and hard before you could ever think of teaching it. Belong to some expensive country club with fancy equipment and tennis courts. Richard and Oracene had none of that. But they weren't going to let that stop them.

HISTORY OF TENNIS

It is widely believed that French monks invented the game of *tenez* in the 11th or 12th century. The tennis that we know of today dates back to 1874, when Welsh inventor and British army officer Major Walter Clopton Wingfield created a new court and rules for the ancient game of tennis. Even though it was originally known as *"lawn tennis,"* the sport is played on a variety of surfaces, including carpet, concrete (the fastest playing surface), asphalt, grass, and clay (a slow playing surface). Men and women play in different categories, unless they are playing in a mixed-doubles tournament.

With no formal instruction, Richard set out to learn tennis by watching videos and reading books. From there, he drafted a 78-page document that outlined just how he planned to help his children achieve greatness. Every day Richard, Oracene, and her three daughters would head to the tennis courts. Together, they practiced **forehands, backhands**, and learned all the drills from Richard's videos.

TENNIS BASICS

Along with serves, the most widely used shots in tennis are the forehand and backhand, also known as **ground strokes**. Here are the basics:

To accomplish a forehand, feet should be placed in the direction from which the ball is traveling. The player swings the racket across the body and toward the desired direction for the shot.

The backhand can be done with either one or two hands. The player positions the racket behind the body for a backswing. As the player extends the racket to the front, the body turns in the direction of the ball. Once coming in contact with the ball, the player moves the ball in the direction that it is supposed to travel.

Two years after Richard watched Virginia Ruzici's historic moment, he and Oracene added a daughter to their blended family. Venus Ebony Starr Williams was born in Lynwood, California on June 17, 1980. Shortly after this, the family moved to Saginaw, Michigan. Just fifteen months after Venus was born, Serena Jameka Williams entered the world on September 26, 1981.

After Serena was born, the family moved back to California, this time to Compton, a largely African American and Hispanic city located in Los Angeles County. Compton was riddled with crime, gangs, and poverty. But, like any city in America, it was and still is filled with people who dare to dream—people like Richard and Oracene.

Tennis would be their ticket out of the inner city, but Richard and Oracene knew that teaching the sport to their children wouldn't be enough to make them champions. The girls had to have drive, passion, and the hunger for greatness.

ABOUT THE GRAND SLAMS

There are four **majors** in tennis, also known as Grand Slams: The Australian Open, the US Open, the French Open, and Wimbledon. A player who wins all four in the same calendar year becomes a Grand Slam champion. In her career, Serena has won 23 Grand Slam singles titles , but she has never won all four tournaments in the same calendar year . . . yet.

If you were to ask Serena what her first memory of tennis was, she would likely not be able to tell you. For Serena, tennis was always there. Like oxygen. Abundant and free.

By the time she could walk, she had a tennis racquet in her hand. And not just any racquet. An adult-sized one. Junior racquets, along with other necessary equipment, would've been too expensive for the large family to afford. So Richard asked private country clubs to donate their used tennis balls and other equipment they no longer needed, and they were happy to oblige.

Family weekends were spent on the public courts of East Rancho Dominguez Park in Compton. The courts were littered with broken glass, nets with holes, and graffiti. Richard would load up a shopping cart full of tennis balls, pack his family in his Volkswagen minibus, and drive all five girls in the family—Yetunde, Isha, Lyndrea, Venus, and Serena—down there.

Gang members lurked around the outskirts. Back then, not many folks actually *used* the tennis courts for their intended purpose. At times, the gang members warned the family that they weren't welcome. They would even pick fights with Richard, sometimes knocking out a few of his teeth. That didn't stop Richard. Every weekend, he returned with his wife and daughters, ready to fight for his rightful place on the courts. Eventually, the gang members realized that he wasn't going away and gave up trying to intimidate him.

In the beginning, young Serena looked on from her stroller while her four older sisters learned the game. But then one sunny afternoon, when she was three, Richard made a special announcement: It was time for Serena to take her first swing.

Serena was tiny compared to the adult-sized racquet she clutched in her hand. She stood up from her stroller, dressed in her white tennis skirt with pink and purple flowers, her hair braided in cornrows, and walked toward her father. Richard placed little Serena a few feet away from the net and told her to swing.

And she did! She sent balls flying onto other courts!

With each missed ball, Richard offered young Serena more words of encouragement, as her family cheered her on.

Oracene's three older daughters didn't take to tennis the way Venus and Serena did, which was fine. The family were devout Jehovah's Witness followers, attending church meetings during the week and Kingdom Hall on Sundays. School studies also kept the Price girls plenty busy.

Life in the Price-Williams household wasn't all tennis. While the Price sisters immersed themselves in school activities, Venus took to track, and Serena learned gymnastics. As a family, they often enjoyed having game nights. Uno was their favorite game, and how fitting, too. Uno is all about trying to get to the finish line, where the last person standing can proclaim victory. Perhaps this was the game that gave Serena her drive to be a winner. But on the flip side, *uno* had a special meaning for the Price-Williams family. In Spanish, *uno* means one—as in being together, united. Richard and Oracene worked hard to instill this, along with a core set of values for their daughters. According to the sisters, priorities were in a very specific order: God, family, education, *then* career.

Early on, Richard and Oracene taught the girls to follow a variety of mantras, special messages that express basic beliefs. You'll find a series of them in this book, inspired by the ones Serena grew up hearing and eventually writing many of her own in a journal. Richard's mantras were often written on large posters that he'd hang around the courts for the girls to see. Messages like *You're a winner* and *Believe in yourself* stayed with Venus and Serena long after they'd leave the court for the night. Oracene's mantras were more verbal, like poetry, softly whispered to the girls in the most special mother-daughter moments. Oracene would remind the girls that no matter what path they chose, so long as they believed

Venus and Serena with their father/coach Richard in Compton, CA

in themselves, their dreams would come true.

Mantras helped both sisters build a champion mindset, so much so that Serena would later keep a journal of her own made-up inspirational messages. Before she would take to the court, Serena would read them over and over, until the words, her focus, and her performance merged as one.

By the time Venus and Serena were six and seven years old, they showed a real passion for the game. So Richard shifted his focus to sharpening their tennis skills. Daily practices began at 6 a.m., before school, followed by late afternoon practices after school. Venus and Serena would hit hundreds of balls, becoming faster and stronger. The sisters grew to love the game so much that they would often cry when practice was over!

Even though local gangs had finally allowed the Williams family to use the courts without interference, the neighborhood wasn't always safe. When Serena was just six years old, she experienced the dangers of Compton in a new, scary way.

One day a car full of gang members cruised down Atlantic Avenue. A window rolled down slowly, and a gun emerged, aimed at rival gang members in the park.

Pop! The first shot rang out.

Serena initially assumed it was a firecracker or balloons popping. But it wasn't the Fourth of July, and there wasn't a birthday party happening in the park.

Pop! Pop! Another round of shots echoed throughout the air.

The girls and their father dropped to the ground. Who knows what they were feeling in that moment? Fearful. Upset. Clinging on to a prayer.

It was a day that the Williams sisters would never forget. Perhaps the flame of hope burned even brighter after that experience. If there was anything that would pull them out of life in a dangerous neighborhood, it was tennis.

To give the girls the best chance at becoming champions, Oracene and Richard intensified their practices to six hours a day. Every day the girls, still in elementary school, would perfect their serves, forehands, and backhands, and compete against Richard's adult friends until, one by one, they beat them all. Venus and Serena were the last two standing. Always. Their serves were so powerful that if you looked away, even for a second, you'd better duck. Those balls flew *fast!*

The Compton courts had served them well, but to be truly great, it was time for something different. It was time for the girls to step outside their comfort zone. The tennis world wouldn't know what hit them.

MANTRA #1:
Believe!

2

STEPPING IT UP

In addition to the six hours of practice a day, which included running, strength training, and stretching, the girls would watch tennis videos for hours to learn how to find an opponent's weakness. This level of study had given Venus and Serena the results that Richard had hoped for. Powerful serves. On-the-mark shots. Quick reaction times. And stamina like nobody's business! (By the age of eight, Venus could run a mile in *under* five minutes!)

Richard and Oracene had done the best they could to teach the girls the game and encourage in them a "can do" attitude. But the time had come for someone more experienced to coach Venus and Serena.

Enter Paul Cohen. In September of 1988, Richard contacted Paul, who was the longtime coach of tennis champ

John McEnroe. Under Cohen's guidance, at just 18 years old in 1979, McEnroe won the mixed doubles at the French Open, and would go on to win at Wimbledon and the US Open in later years. Cohen invited Richard and the girls to his tennis estate in Brentwood, California—a mere twenty-three miles from Compton, but a world away from the cracked concrete and scattered glass of their neighborhood courts.

TENNIS BASICS

In tennis, two opposing players play as **singles**, where men and women compete in separate, same-gender tournaments. Tennis can also be played in pairs by same-gender (men's and women's doubles) or **mixed doubles**, where men and women play as a team.

Once Cohen started hitting around with the girls on the court, he was impressed by their athletic abilities. Especially Serena's. He remembers her as the strongest seven-year-old he'd ever met. As for Venus, Cohen saw a potential champion in her as well. Cohen's plan? Train them to attack so that no matter who was standing on the other side of the net, Venus and Serena would annihilate them from the very first serve.

During this time, Richard also signed Venus up for the United States Tennis Association. The USTA would give nine-year-old Venus the opportunity to play outside of the Compton courts and in a more competitive arena. Richard felt that at that age she was ready. Serena, on the other hand, wasn't quite ready. Yet. Richard's plan was for her to play in less competitive recreational leagues.

WHAT IS THE USTA?

Every sport has its own professional league, made up of rules and regulations for players to follow. In many cases, these leagues have organized teams that play each other in various games. Basketball has the NBA (National Basketball Association). Football has the NFL (National Football League). In tennis, there is the United Stated Tennis Association. Originally named the United States National Lawn Tennis Association (that's a mouthful!), the acronym has changed many times since the league was established in 1881, when it was just a small group of New York City tennis club members. The word *national* was dropped from the acronym in 1920, followed by "lawn" in 1975, to simply become USTA. The mission of the USTA is to promote the game of tennis, while expanding its popularity.

The USTA tournaments took place all around southern California, and it was clear at these events that tennis was not a very diverse sport. Oftentimes, Venus was the only black player in the junior tournaments. People stared. People whispered. People treated her poorly. Because what could a little black girl from Compton possibly know about tennis? Especially one who had trained on public courts scattered with broken glass, while the other emerging tennis stars had trained at private clubs? But the second a game started, Venus showed them exactly what she knew and what she could do. She dominated the courts with **serves** that beelined past her opponents, just as Cohen and Richard had trained her to do.

TENNIS BASICS

Serve: Tennis tournaments begin with a serve. To serve, a player tosses the ball upward, raising the racket, and hitting the ball over the net.

Serena sat on the sidelines, proud of her big sister but with a fire burning up inside her. The recreational leagues just weren't cutting it for her. Serena was determined to compete, just like Venus. If her father wouldn't sign her up, then she would have to take matters into her own hands.

One day, Serena filled out an application to enter an upcoming USTA tournament. She told no one—not even Venus, which was probably hard because they weren't just sisters, they were best friends. During one of Venus's matches, Serena snuck off to another court to play her own match. By the time Richard found out, it was too late. He had no other choice but to sit on the sidelines, switching back and forth between courts, as each daughter clobbered their opponents until they were the last two standing. This was Richard's worst nightmare come true!

Venus, who was older, taller, and more powerful than Serena, won the tournament. Serena was heartbroken, but Venus gave her the trophy to make her feel better. That's how things went in the Williams household—family over *everything*. It was in that moment that Richard decided to move Serena out of the recreational leagues and let Serena play on the junior level in one age category below Venus. There was no denying either girl's skill. Venus moved up to the 12 and under league, winning 63 out of 63 games. Serena remained in the 10 and under league, winning 46 games and only losing 3.

Cohen's coaching, alongside Richard's, helped the girls improve so much that, eventually, Cohen would invite tennis pros John McEnroe and Pete Sampras to come watch the girls practice in Brentwood. Both McEnroe and Sampras were trained by Cohen. Venus hit a few balls with them and she would later tell the media that she felt as if she could've beaten McEnroe fair and square!

Venus's success in the USTA laid the foundation for the Williams sisters' greatness. In 1990, at age 10, Venus won the Junior Sectional Championships in southern California—her 17th singles title in *less* than a year! This catapulted her to the 14 and under division, and tennis fans put Venus—the tall 10-year-old who played like a teenager—on their radar.

Who were these sisters from Compton taking the court by storm? The media buzzed with excitement, but the spotlight was mostly on Venus. Not Serena, even though she, too, was ranked #1 in her age division.

TENNIS BASICS

Throughout this book, you'll find the words *rank*, *seeded*, and *unseeded* used quite a bit.

Ranking is a part of life. In school, your grades may be ranked against those of other students. This is why many graduating classes have a valedictorian (the student with the highest grade point average) and a salutatorian (the student with the second highest grade point average). It's the same deal in sports. All great athletes work hard in hopes of reaching the #1 rank. As you read, you'll learn the rankings of many tennis players, in addition to how (and sometimes why) their rankings have changed over the years.

In professional tennis, specifically for an event like Wimbledon, ranks are looked at to determine seeds. (And no, we're not talking about plants!) Seeding is a system used to make sure that top players don't meet in early rounds of a tournament. For now, 32 seeds (32 top players) are ranked for the Grand Slams, though this number may change to 16 in 2019. Top seeds are considered the strongest players. They compete first against lower seeded and unseeded players. The final two players remaining—supposedly the best—compete against one another at the end.

On July 3, 1990, the *New York Times* ran an article on Venus, highlighting her success. She was the only undefeated player in her league. Even more extraordinary was that she was an African American kid dominating a sport largely played by white people. The article predicted that Venus would reach the same heights as the greats, known by first name only—Billie Jean, Martina, and Steffi. According to the *Times*, Venus fit right in.

Sponsors began lining up: Reebok, Wilson, Prince. All athletic companies that wanted to offer better clothing and equipment to the rising 10-year-old tennis star.

Where was Serena during all this? Practicing, of course. Pushing harder, her own eyes filled with hope and dreams as Venus climbed the ranks to the top. Serena wasn't in the spotlight like Venus was, but she wasn't far behind.

In May 1991, Richard contacted renowned coach Rick Macci in Florida. Richard invited Macci out to Compton to see his daughters play. Having seen the *New York Times* article on Venus, along with a second article that ran in the *Times* featuring both Venus and Serena, Macci decided to take a trip to see what the hype was all about.

ON A FIRST-NAME BASIS

Some athletes are so popular that people know them by first name only. Let's see if you recognize some of these favorites:

LEBRON JAMES

LEBRON (1984–)
Basketball MVP, current small forward for the Los Angeles Lakers

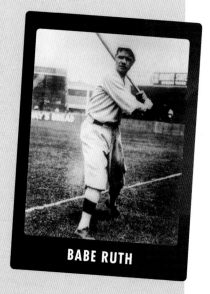
BABE RUTH

BABE (1895–1948)
Major league baseball player for the New York Yankees

SHALENE (1981–):
American long distance runner, record holder, winner of the New York Marathon, and four-time Olympian

SHALENE FLANAGAN

PELÉ (1940–):
Retired soccer player from Brazil, and three-time World Cup champion, often regarded as the greatest soccer player of all time

PELÉ

VENUS (1980–):
Does she *really* need an introduction?

VENUS WILLIAMS

When Macci arrived, he was shocked at the appearance of the courts that the girls practiced on in Compton. How could a champion be made here? And when Richard began running balls with the girls, Macci wasn't impressed. He felt that Richard didn't have the coaching chops, which was an easy assumption, given that Richard never really played tennis growing up. Also, Venus and Serena showed that they had talent, but for Macci they didn't demonstrate anything truly unique. After all, Macci was a trainer to the stars! His latest protégé, Jennifer Capriati, had made her professional debut at the age of 13.

An hour into the practice, the girls took a rest. Venus exited the gate, placed her hands on the concrete, lifted her long legs to the sky, and began to walk. On her *hands*! She walked about ten feet before standing and doing a series of backwards cartwheels.

Now, *that* got his attention! Venus's athleticism was like nothing he'd ever seen, and that's when it clicked for him. After seeing that display, Macci whispered to Richard that they might be looking at the next female Michael Jordan.

Richard quickly corrected Macci, saying that they were looking at the next *two*!

The question was no longer *if* Macci would train

Richard practices with Serena in Compton, CA.

Venus and Serena but how fast they could move to Florida and get started. Macci would train and sponsor both girls, put the family up in a motor home, pay for a golf club membership and a variety of non–tennis-related classes, in exchange for a single promise: When the girls reached pro level, Macci would earn a small percentage of their earnings. That was an offer Richard couldn't refuse.

Soon enough, the girls would kiss Compton good-bye and make their way to the sunshine state. But first, Richard would make a decision that would shock the entire tennis community.

ATTENTION READERS:

We interrupt this book with an important message:
If you want to become a great tennis player, like Serena,
here's what you should do:

1. Play in junior tournaments against other pros-in-training.

2. Create buzz in the tennis community.

3. Eventually advance to the pros.

After all, this is how Serena became the G.O.A.T., right?

Not quite.

BEFORE SERENA . . .

We can't have a book about the G.O.A.T. without mentioning some of the great African American athletes who came before Serena Williams. Their success paved the way for Serena to soar, but most of all it was their sacrifice that would eventually open doors for all people of color to play tennis:

ORA MAE WASHINGTON

ORA MAE WASHINGTON

Some people credit **Ora Mae Washington** as the "mother of tennis." She played in the American Tennis Association (ATA) from 1924 to 1937. With her prowess and athleticism, Washington could have easily played for the USTA. But those tournaments were held at private clubs. The only way black people were allowed inside was if they were maids or cooks.

Washington took her talents to the ATA, a black-owned association formed in response to the USTA's racist policies. She won eight ATA women's singles titles from 1929 to 1937, along with 12 straight women's doubles titles from 1925 to 1936. During the years of 1939, 1946, and 1947, Washington also captured mixed doubles titles.

Tennis wasn't her only sport. Washington played the position of center for the Philadelphia Tribune's women's basketball team. As a powerful ball player, Washington traveled the United States playing in games against people of all races and genders.

In 1976, she was inducted into the Black Athletes Hall of Fame, five years after her death. In 2018, she was inducted into the Naismith Memorial Basketball Hall of Fame.

ALTHEA GIBSON

ALTHEA GIBSON

Althea Gibson made history in not one, but two sports. She was the first African American woman to tour on the LPGA (Ladies Professional Golf Association) golf circuit and, more importantly, she was the first African American player to win a Grand Slam title in tennis.

Born August 25, 1927 in South Carolina, she moved to Harlem, New York at a young age with her family. There, her love of tennis flourished, but there was a huge problem standing in her way. African Americans were largely shut out of all-white tennis tournaments. As a result, Gibson competed for the black-owned American Tennis Association and became a champion.

As she moved through the ranks, the racism and discrimination that Gibson endured was so bad that she considered leaving the sport. Everyone could see her talent and skill, but still the color of her skin prevented her from playing in the USTA.

In 1949, former tennis great Alice Marble wrote a scathing article for *American Lawn Tennis Magazine*, criticizing the sport for denying Gibson a chance to play in the world's elite tournaments.

Fortunately, Gibson did not give up. Over the course of her career, she

- Became the first black woman to compete for the US National Championships in 1950
- Became the first black player at Wimbledon in 1951
- Won the French singles championship and the French doubles championship in 1956, as well as the doubles championship at Wimbledon that same year

- Became the first black woman to win the women's singles title at the Wimbledon Open in 1957

By the time Gibson retired from tennis in 1958, the question no longer remained if African Americans deserved a place in the tennis world.

ARTHUR ASHE

Born in Richmond, Virginia, on July 10, 1943, Arthur Ashe was a leading tennis pioneer.

Much like Althea Gibson, Ashe faced segregation and roadblocks due to his race.

Ashe had a successful run as a junior with the black-owned American Tennis Association before advancing to the USLTA where he became the first African American junior to earn a national ranking. His achievements included:

ARTHUR ASHE

- Becoming the first black male winner of the US Open in 1968, the Australian Open in 1970, and Wimbledon in 1975

- Becoming the first black player selected to play in the Davis Cup in the United States. He played in a total of 10 Davis Cup teams during the 1960s and 1970s. During this time, Ashe won five championships.

- The Arthur Ashe Stadium in Flushing Meadows, New York being named in his honor.

ZINA GARRISON

ZINA GARRISON

By the time Venus and Serena began playing tennis, Zina Garrison was a force to be reckoned with!

Zina was born in Houston, Texas on November 16, 1963. Like Venus and Serena, Zina also came from a large family; she had six siblings. She began playing tennis at 10 years old at the MacGregor Park Tennis Program.

Prior to beginning her professional career in 1982, Zina had won three major tournaments, and became the 1981 International Tennis Federation Junior of the Year. She would go on earn a gold medal in the 1988 Olympics in South Korea, three Grand Slam mixed doubles titles, and her most distinguished victory of all: reaching the finals at a Grand Slam tournament—at Wimbledon—in 1990. The last time an African American had done that was in 1958, when Althea Gibson reached the finals at the US Open.

Zina was certainly a contemporary role model for Venus and Serena Williams.

3

A GUTSY MOVE

Tradition shaker. Rule breaker. History maker. Richard Williams was all these things, and so were his daughters. Shortly after meeting with Rick Macci, Richard made a gutsy move that shocked the whole tennis community: He pulled Venus and Serena out of junior tennis.

Some of the best players started as champs in the junior circuit and went on to be professional tennis powerhouses: Pete Sampras, Andre Agassi, Monica Seles, and many others. Even Zina Garrison played junior tennis before claiming Althea Gibson's spotlight! This was the way of the tennis world. You paid your dues, on the court, with the best-of-the-best up-and-comers.

UP-AND-COMERS

Before they were pros, they were juniors on the rise . . .

PETE SAMPRAS
 USA

Junior Claim to Fame:

- Undefeated in 56 sets and won the title of Southern Section CIF (California Interscholastic Federation) 4–A in 1986 at the age of 15

- Turned pro at 16 years old

ANDRE AGASSI
 USA

Junior Claim to Fame:

- 1982 National Indoor Boy 14's Double Champ

- Turned pro at 16 years old

MONICA SELES
 YUGOSLAVIA

Junior Claim to Fame:

- Won the Junior Orange Bowl in Miami, Florida at only 11 years old!

- Turned pro at 15 years old

So why did Richard pull his girls out of junior tennis? If you recall, nothing was more important to the Williams family than family, faith, and education. Career was at the bottom of the priority list. Venus and Serena were straight-A students and Richard wanted to keep it that way. To him, there was too much pressure in junior tennis. The would-be pros would be crisscrossing the country, spending days and sometimes weeks away from their family. That kind of lifestyle wasn't going to work for the tight-knit, Price-Williams family.

In September 1991, the Williams family piled into their new minibus, leaving Serena's oldest sister, Yetunde, in California. Yetunde was already in college, studying to become a nurse. The move left Serena with mixed emotions: excited to begin a new life in Del Ray, Florida, where she and Venus would officially become students of Rick Macci's, yet sad to leave her big sister, her fiercest protector behind.

Their training began immediately. In addition to training on the court, Macci enrolled the girls in taekwondo, boxing, gymnastics, and even ballet. These extra classes weren't for fun (even though they *were* fun and the girls had a blast), but a part of Macci's strategy. Venus and Serena wanted to become tennis warriors and Macci wanted to do everything in his power to make that happen. That meant signing them up for other sports that would help improve their strength, flexibility, and control.

The publicity increased after this bold move. The girls had already been featured in the *New York Times*, *People* magazine, and *Trans World Sport TV*. The media fashioned Venus into a legend, even though she was no longer competing. Between 1991 and 1994, the sisters trained under Rick Macci's masterful eye and perfected their game away from the eyes of the public. During this time, Serena and Venus were pulled out of seventh and eighth grade, respectively, to be homeschooled by Oracene.

Serena, Oracene, and Venus

In 1995, a new rule in women's tennis forced Venus to make a hard-and-fast decision, much to the dismay of her father. For 43 years, the Women's Tennis Association had placed young prodigies like Monica Seles, Chris Evert, and Martina Hingis on a pedestal. But tennis star Jennifer Capriati's career path forced the WTA to reexamine their values. At age 13, Capriati played in her first tournament, to the delight of the media.

DID YOU KNOW?

The WTA was established in 1973 by Billie Jean King as a primary organization that manages women's professional tennis tournaments. Stay tuned to learn more about Billie Jean King's WTA legacy!

But by 18, Capriati was burned out and a drug addict in need of rehabilitation. Critics blamed the WTA for allowing tennis players to turn pro too young and making unhealthy demands of them. As a result, the WTA created the "Capriati Rule" to prevent any future player from experiencing the pressure that caused Jennifer Capriati's promising career to take a wrong turn. This new rule raised the pro age for girls to 16. The new rule would go into effect at the *end* of 1995. For years, Richard was adamant about his daughters not turning pro until they were 18. For him, the pressure was not worth

The Williams sisters at Serena's pro debut

it. But for Venus, the only way to go was up, and Richard knew there was nothing he could do to stand in her way.

Making the decision on her own, Venus decided to turn pro at the age of 14, ahead of the new WTA restrictions. Serena, a year younger than her sister, would have to wait.

On Halloween of 1994, the time had come for Venus to finally make a public appearance. The Williams family and Rick Macci headed to Oakland, where Venus would play in the Bank of West Classic tournament. For the 1993 tournament there were only about 23 media outlets present. But a year later, 252 outlets showed up for what they believed would be one for the books!

Dressed in a nameless tennis outfit from the JCPenney® clearance rack and holding a nameless tennis racket, Venus Williams, the girl from the wrong side of the tennis court, stepped up to play #57-ranked Shaun Stafford. With a serve of 115 mph, Venus stepped all over Stafford, winning in straight sets, 6–3, 6–4. The media went nuts!

TENNIS BASICS

Tennis matches are composed of two to three sets, with six games in each set. The player who wins two out of three sets wins the match. If each player wins one set, playing a third set determines the winner.

But then it was time to play Spanish tennis pro, Arantxa Sánchez Vicario. In the beginning, Venus had a 6–3, 3–1 lead, and it looked like she was on her way to a resounding victory. But in the end, Sánchez Vicario won the last nine games of the match. At just 14 years old, Venus had made her professional debut—and had experienced both the winning and losing ends of the competition. Some would've considered it a bust, but in Venus's mind, she was ready for takeoff!

That one tournament was enough to send executives from every major sports apparel company knocking on the Williams's door. Surely, the kid from Compton could use brand-name apparel to play televised tennis events. On May 22, 1995, Venus signed a five-year deal with Reebok for $12 million. And so began the rise of the Williams empire! The family from Compton, with hardworking parents and even harder-working children, had never seen that many zeros in their life!

Richard purchased a 40-acre compound in Palm Beach, Florida and had tennis courts installed, complete with the large posters of the mantras he would display on the Compton courts. The girls stopped homeschooling and enrolled in a private school, Driftwood Academy. Richard and Oracene hired private tutors to help the girls maintain high grade point averages. They even learned Italian and French, which would come in handy later on when they would travel the world for tournaments.

Shortly after the Williams landed their fortune, Richard made another gutsy move: He fired Rick Macci. Ouch!

Experts were skeptical of his decision. Rick Macci was responsible for coaching Venus to reach her professional debut, and Serena, too, who had another year to wait before she could turn pro. But Richard, ever so stubborn, ever so focused, felt he knew what was best for his daughters. He would return as their full-time trainer and coach. For all of 1995 and 1996, that's exactly what he did.

By October 1995, it was time for Venus's little sister to step out of the shadows. Would Serena live up to the hype that was already built for Venus? Or could she do the unthinkable and do even more? Could she step out of her big sister's shadow to make her own name, and maybe even make history?

4

TURNING PRO

Imagine 10 years of preparation to become the greatest of all time. Ten years of practicing six days a week, six hours a day. And then picture those dreams, the visions of championship glory, finally yours for the taking. How would you feel? Excited? Prepared? Nervous? Perhaps a combination of all three?

The skies were gloomy on October 27, 1995. Clouds threatened to release a series of storms. Every practice, every mantra, every whispered hope, had led to this moment: Serena Williams was finally turning pro.

Serena and Richard headed to Philadelphia International Airport, where they would travel to the Bell Challenge in Quebec City, Canada. The Bell Challenge wasn't Wimbledon by any means. There would be no crowds of potential fans, no blinding flashes from the hundreds of media outlets that had shown up for Venus's Bank of West Classic. It didn't matter, though, because this was a day that Serena would celebrate, even if the WTA and her parents didn't necessarily agree with her decision to enter.

Serena's road to her professional debut was a lot less flashy and definitely rockier than Venus's. After the WTA enforced a 15-year-old age limit, Venus was one of the last 14-year-olds to play a mainstream event in 1995. As Serena's 14th birthday approached, she knew she had to take matters into her own hands. It's the same heightened determination she had all those years ago when she signed up for junior tennis behind Richard's back. Serena tried to score a wild card entry into the Bank of the West Classic, the same tournament where Venus made her splashy debut in 1994. When that didn't work, she filed an antitrust lawsuit against the WTA because the new age restrictions would prevent her from turning pro when she wanted to, which was immediately. Serena didn't want to wait. She believed she was ready right then.

In filing the lawsuit, she asked the WTA to allow her to be an exception to the new rule. Serena made these sneaky moves without enlisting legal assistance from the family's attorney, Kevin Davis, nor her parents. Richard and Oracene weren't all that surprised. After all, Serena was no stranger to going after what she wanted, no matter what the consequence. Richard and Oracene urged Serena to drop the lawsuit (and she did), but they discovered a loophole in the WTA's age restriction. If the Bell Challenge would offer Serena a wild card entry into their Tier III tournament, she could still turn pro. The tournament wasn't nearly as popular as other major events, but it was a foot in the door. A small victory!

So when Serena arrived at the Philadelphia International Airport, she wanted to celebrate all her hard work, all those years of being in the shadows that led to her crowning moment. And what better way to do that than with a little shopping? While waiting to board the plane, Serena and Richard checked out the souvenir shops at the airport.

With her newly purchased gifts in hand, Serena and Richard headed to the gate to catch their plane. When they got there, panic set in. The cabin doors had closed! The plane was already in the air! The worst part of all? Serena's racquets were stored beneath the plane! How could they have lost track of time?

The Bell Challenge was set to begin the next day, October 28. The nightmare only got worse as Richard and Serena traveled through four different airports before they finally reached Canada. Most of Serena's tennis equipment got lost in the shuffle. They arrived in Quebec City in the late hours of the night. Serena missed her chance to practice for the next day's event. All she could do was get to her hotel, fall asleep, and pray for a miracle the next day.

• • •

The next morning proved to be no better. Instead of a large stadium, Serena competed on a regular practice court at a tennis club, with a smoky bar and an ice cream store just one floor above her. Approximately 50 spectators showed up for the event, equal parts interested, equal parts without a care in the world.

Serena stepped on the court to face 18-year-old Annie Miller. Miller, whose career would end abruptly at the age of 21, had never won a WTA title. Perhaps, on that day, things were set to change.

Serena was four years younger than Miller, and definitely not as advanced. Miller played on the junior circuit—unlike Serena, whose father had pulled her out early. The odds were in Miller's favor from the beginning. Sure, there were flashes of Serena's power and talent, much like what was written of her and Venus in the *New*

York Times. But Serena's reaction times were off. She chased balls, and missed shots. In the end, Miller beat Serena 6–1, 6–1 at an event that the tennis world barely considered noteworthy.

In less than an hour, it was all over. Serena's prize money? A meager $240. Annie Miller's? A whopping $1,750! Both amounts were small change compared to Venus's $12 million Reebok deal.

The Bell Challenge was supposed to be Serena's "Cinderella" moment. We all know how the story goes: Once upon a time, there lived a girl who hid in the shadows of her sister, and dreamed of becoming the belle of the ball.

But as everybody knows, fairy tales don't always have smooth roads to a happy ending. The best fairy tales are like roller coasters—full of adversities that the main character needs to overcome before she can finally save the day or win the crown.

Defeated and deflated, Serena Williams headed home without her own crowning victory. She wouldn't play another tournament for the next 18 months.

You might think that the Quebec City fiasco is a valid reason to discredit Serena as the G.O.A.T. Nothing about her debut screams "greatest of all time," but to be great, you have to fail a bit too. Otherwise, how else will you get better? Maybe Serena knew that this was the hidden secret to becoming the G.O.A.T. So she made a promise to herself: By her next professional showing, she would be ready. Serena Williams would prove to herself that she could build on failure and show the tennis world what she was capable of.

MANTRA #2

Failure is a main ingredient in the recipe for success!

TEENAGE SERENA

What did Serena do after a major career disappointment? She did what most teenagers might do after receiving a bad grade on a test:

Serena with her dog Jackie

1. She went to school, studied really hard, and made good grades. (Because tennis is an international sport, both Serena and Venus learned how to speak Italian and French!)

2. She hung out at the mall with her sisters, because a little retail therapy is good for the soul. (Her favorite store was Mervyn's!)

3. She played with her dogs.

4. She looked forward to getting her driver's license.

5. She watched a LOT of *Golden Girls* episodes.

In lots of ways, Serena was like other teenagers, except she had this unusual passion that took up six hours a day, six days a week of her time: tennis. From the moment she was born, it was the air she inhaled and exhaled. The loss at the Bell Challenge shook Serena's confidence. Because of it, she lost a bit of her motivation, and found herself sitting on the couch watching television when she wasn't playing tennis. And that's okay. Everyone needs a break every once in a while, especially after a huge upset. But was she going to allow this one loss to make her give up on her tennis dreams? Not a chance.

5

ON THE RISE

By late 1995, Serena was officially a professional tennis player, but only because of that one appearance in Quebec. In reality, she had realized that she was an amateur in need of practice. The biggest lesson Serena learned was that if she wanted to be a champion, a true G.O.A.T., she would have to fight for it. Gone were the days of little-kid tournaments back in southern California, where she defeated almost every girl across the net. Here, on the professional stage, Serena would have to earn her place. She would have to take all that she'd learned and use it as fuel to push her forward.

Serena did not play in any WTA matches in 1996. Instead, she practiced harder than she ever had before. Also during this time, Venus and Serena together stepped up their practice by playing doubles. Growing up, they'd often practiced this way, and Serena loved having her sister on her side of the net, as opposed to the other side. It was a comforting reminder of their childhood days in Compton, where in the middle of the night, Serena would crawl into her big sister's bed after a bad dream.

Fast-forward to 1997.

Serena played a limited schedule where her game still showed inconsistencies. Because of this, she did not advance to qualifying rounds during three tournaments and her WTA rank showed that clearly: #440. A whopping 439 places away from the rank she'd always hoped to be.

In March 1997, Serena's second professional tournament was at Indian Wells, in Palm Springs, in her home state of California. There, she played French pro Alexia Dechaume-Balleret and was clobbered 6–4, 6–0.

But all wasn't lost. Venus and Serena would finally play their first doubles tournament. At 15 years old, with very little professional experience, Serena found her strength by playing with her sister. By this point, Venus was really making a name for herself in the tennis world. Playing doubles at Indian Wells was just what Serena needed to elevate her game and status. Serena and Venus advanced all the way to the quarter finals, and though they eventually lost, to Lindsay Davenport and Natasha

Serena Williams and Venus Williams at USTA National Tennis Center, in Flushing Meadows, NY

Zvereva, in a 6–3, 6–0 upset, people were finally starting to notice Serena as Serena—not just "Venus's little sister."

Venus and Serena would go on to win their first championship playing doubles at Oklahoma City the next year, in 1998. Serena was just 16 years old, and Venus was 17. Both were still very young, still quite inexperienced, and that showed in their doubles ranking: 192.

The sisters were raised to believe that not everything was about winning. That in the midst of failing, there was room for learning, growth, and success.

They took those lessons and spilled them out on the court of Oklahoma City, where they celebrated an unexpected quarterfinals win over African American player, Katrina Adams, and the WTA "Newcomer of the Year," Debbie Graham. While this would mark Serena and Venus's very first tour championship, it would also serve as a reminder of Richard and Oracene's greatest mantra: Family first. This is where Serena found her confidence and strength.

The win at Oklahoma City was just what Serena, now a full-time pro, needed. There would be no more hiding, no more missed tournaments, no more binge-watching *Golden Girls* (though she still made time occasionally for her favorite show!). Serena Jameka Williams was all-in. Building on the confidence that Venus and her family helped instill in her, Serena was officially ready to claim her place in the spotlight.

CAREER HIGHLIGHTS

When it comes to Serena's accomplishments on the court, there simply aren't enough pages to cover them all. So we've put some of her career highlights into a "time line." Actually, make that a few roller coasters. Because that's what Serena's career has been: plenty of career highs, marked by a few low moments in between. Through it all, Serena has shown that she is someone who isn't afraid to fail and rise again. These are the qualities that make her a true G.O.A.T.

ROLLER COASTER TIME LINE
PART I

FUN(NY) FACT!

At just 16 years old, Serena and her father flew to Los Angeles to meet with representatives of Puma. In hopes that Serena would learn how to negotiate a sponsorship deal, he insisted that Serena stay for the entire meeting. The meeting began around noon and Serena was excited to hear all about what Puma could offer to boost her career. Hours later, however, around midnight, while an offer of $12 million was being negotiated, Serena found herself asleep at the table.

1998 Serena enters her first Grand Slam tournament, the Australian Open, and loses to Venus in the second round.

1997 The marketing offers pour in! Serena lands an unprecedented $12 million deal with Puma. The athletic wear company had never sponsored anyone in tennis before. Serena is the FIRST!

1997 In March, Serena and Venus play doubles at Indian Wells. They advance to the quarterfinals before losing to Lindsay Davenport and Natasha Zvereva.

1997 At the Ameritech Cup in November, Serena reaches the semifinals, beating top 10 players Mary Pierce (#7) and Monica Seles (#4), before losing to Lindsay Davenport. Serena is now ranked #304.

1995 Serena makes her professional debut in October at the Bell Challenge in Quebec City, Canada. She loses to Annie Miller, a little-known tennis player, ranked 149th in the world.

1998 Serena graduates from high school in May, a year early. Nine months after her professional tennis debut, Serena now ranks in the top 20. Moving from the bottom of the ranks to the top has never been done before. Not even by her sister, Venus!

2000 After recovering from tendonitis of the knee, Serena faces Venus at Wimbledon in July. Venus defeats Serena in the semifinals, going on to defeat Lindsay Davenport in the finals and becoming the first African American to win since Arthur Ashe in 1975.

2000 In September, Venus and Serena play in doubles tournaments at the Summer Olympics in Sydney, Australia, and bring home the gold for the United States!

1999 Serena beats Martina Hingis in the finals of the US Open. It is her first Grand Slam singles title. Serena becomes the first African American woman to win a Grand Slam singles title since Althea Gibson in 1958. Bill Clinton, the 42nd president of the United States, personally calls Serena to congratulate her. She finishes the year with a win-loss percentage of 85.42%.

1998 Serena debuts at Wimbledon in June. She falls behind in the third round and pulls out of the singles tournament due to a knee injury.

1999 In June at the French Open, Serena and Venus make history as the first sisters to win a Grand Slam doubles title, defeating Anna Kournikova and Martina Hingis.

1999 Serena enters the top 10 of the WTA, ranking at #7.

1999 Serena returns to Indian Wells in March. At just 17 years old, Serena, with just one WTA singles title to her name, defeats 29-year-old Steffi Graf, who has 106 WTA singles titles, including 22 Grand Slam singles titles.

2001 Indian Wells. Palm Springs, California. What is supposed to be a crowd-pleasing showdown between Venus and Serena turns out to be a memory that Serena won't soon forget. . .

MANTRA #3

Rumors travel,
swift like wind.
Only truth remains,
sure as sunrise,
coming back again.

6

INDIAN WELLS BRINGS THE HEAT

Rumors are funny things. Hushed words, built mostly of lies. Stories that begin with a single line, with each person adding the next, until it becomes a mountain. Too big and at times, too hard to break.

Perhaps that's what happened on March 15, 2001 at the Indian Wells tournament in Palm Springs, California. What should have been a joyous event for Serena began with a rumor.

It was no secret that while raising Serena and Venus to become champions, Richard did all he could to prevent his daughters from competing against each other. That worked when they were little girls, playing junior tennis in different age categories. When they turned pro, it became almost impossible. In singles matches, playing other opponents, both Serena and Venus held their own. However, when they played each other, most described their game as timid and disappointing at best. If you recall, Serena had always been in Venus's shadow, which was, in many ways, a great motivator for Serena. She adored her sister, and even though Serena loved to win, Venus proved herself to be victorious over Serena many times. Prior to March 2001, Venus defeated Serena in the Australian Open, the Italian Open, the Lipton International Players Championships, and Wimbledon. Serena upset Venus once in the finals of the Grand Slam Cup in late 1999.

Over the years, the rumors began to swirl. Did Richard decide beforehand who would win a match, if Venus and Serena were the last two standing? This pressing question was on everyone's mind as the announcer at Indian Wells got on the loudspeaker, four minutes before the start of the tournament, and proclaimed:

Venus Williams has withdrawn from the tournament due to injury.

Truth be told, Venus informed the tournament trainer that she wouldn't be able to compete early that morning because of tendonitis. Those were the rules according to the WTA. Inform the trainer well in advance. This would give the director enough time to tell the fans and reschedule another match in its place.

But that's not how things went down.

Seventeen thousand fans sat in the stands. Swarms of media were everywhere. Advertising sponsors were lined up, having already poured loads of money to promote the Williams versus Williams showdown. People stared at each other, confusion growing on their faces. The accusations started as a whisper, but soon grew to loud, angry boos.

As Richard walked and Venus hobbled to their seats to watch Serena play, the boos grew louder. The words grew harsher. Someone yelled at Serena to go back to Compton. Others threatened her. People hurled disgusting, racial slurs at the Williams family.

Serena stepped onto the court holding a bouquet of flowers, a tradition at Indian Wells, and the angry chants reached their loudest. The ugliness of their words poured down on Serena, so hard, so fast, she didn't know what to do. She had played at Indian Wells before and had a good showing, defeating Steffi Graf, a player so good and so respected that some might argue she is the G.O.A.T. of tennis. Serena's last appearance at Indian Wells was met with cheers and a well-mannered audience. This was her home state, after all.

Because of its location, the whole family—Richard, Oracene, Yetunde, Lyndrea, and Isha—was able to attend that day. Being there held a special place in Serena's heart because her big, happy family could be together, which was rare. They stayed at a local hotel and got to spend quality time together. But in that moment, Serena did not feel like she was home at all. All she could see was a sea of angry faces, most of them older and white, calling her racist names and telling her that she (and her family) were not welcome.

Sadly, no efforts were made to quiet down the crowd. WTA officials sat on the sidelines, with their mouths fixed open, yet they said nothing as the angry fans spewed hateful words at the teen phenomenon.

Serena was set to face Kim Clijsters, a young Belgian player whom the WTA named Newcomer of the Year in 2000. Kim was just 17 years old, younger than Serena by two years. Serena had a leg up in the experience department, too. She had beaten Kim in the US Open in 1999, and again in 2000 at Indian Wells. Kim was ranked #14 to Serena's #7. And for Kim, this was her very first Tier I event.

Serena had this in the bag. Or so she thought.

As she tried to block out the boos from the audience, Kim arrived on the court. Quickly, the angry boos, meant for Serena, changed into loud, sweeping cheers and a standing ovation as Kim waltzed in, flower bouquet in hand.

Serena kicked off the tournament with her signature weapon: her serve. Planted on the hard surface, her front foot pointed toward the right of the net, her back foot aimed right at the baseline, gripping the racquet as if it were a hammer, Serena swung . . . and missed. Overjoyed, the crowd burst into laughter and cheers!

For the first game, Kim scored four straight points: an **ace**, a backhand into the net, followed by a forehand. Kim Clijsters was a girl on fire! Serena, on the other hand, *felt* the fire—the searing heat from the crowd who booed her every move, yet praised the younger, more inexperienced player.

TENNIS BASICS

An **ace** earns the player a single point against his or her opponent when the opponent fails to hit the ball after a serve.

Kim continued like this for three more points, bringing her total to seven. Serena's concentration wavered. Would she remain shaken like this through the whole game? Would she allow the hate of others to fill her with doubt?

Somehow, she was able to break Kim in the next game, bringing the score to 4–3 in Serena's favor. But Kim rallied back in the second set, bringing on more cheers from the audience.

During the changeover, Serena grabbed her towel and pressed her face into it to cry. In that moment, winning seemed impossible for the tough girl from Compton who had been born and bred for victory. But then something came over Serena. Images of an African American heroine appeared in Serena's mind: Althea Gibson. She had been through far worse. Denied reservations in hotels during tournaments. All because of the color of her skin. Slept in her car instead, while her white opponents enjoyed the comfort of a hotel bed. All because of the color of her skin. Still, Althea went on to win several titles and broke barriers on and off the court.

Serena knew Althea's story, and she realized that she stood on the shoulders of Althea Gibson. There was no other choice but to fight back. The battle wasn't between Serena and Kim. This was now a battle against injustice.

The turnaround was fiery and immediate. Serena unleashed a powerful 114 mph bullet for an ace! The angry mob roared, but for some strange reason, Serena heard none of it. With the score at 30–40, Kim landed a **dropshot** that Serena reached, much to the dismay of the crowd. Serena took the next five games and won the match 4–6, 6–4, 6–2.

TENNIS BASICS

A **dropshot** in tennis is also known as a specialty shot. A good dropshot will rise high above the net and land close to your opponent's side of the net, making it difficult for your opponent to fire back. The best time to serve a dropshot is when your opponent is far from the net, in the back of the court. The next time you play tennis, trick your opponent with a dropshot and they won't know what hit 'em!

Overcome with emotion, Serena could no longer hold back her tears. But this time, they were tears of joy. She ran to hug her father and Venus, while the crowd continued to boo.

But none of that was important. Serena made a promise to herself: she would never return to Indian Wells again. It didn't matter that it was a mandatory tournament on the tour. It didn't matter that the WTA could fine her for not showing up to future matches there. What mattered was the message. What would future African American junior tennis players think if she kept playing at this tournament after how she'd been treated? That it's okay for people to mistreat you, even when you've done nothing wrong? That wasn't the role model Serena wanted to be.

She wanted to be strong, powerful, great. Serena lifted her chin to the sky, and perhaps said a heartfelt

Serena hugs her father as Venus waits in the back after her victory over Kim Clijsters at Tennis Masters Series in Indian Wells, CA.

thank-you to Althea Gibson as she left the stadium with her trophy, check, and dignity in hand. Because when you are that exceptional, that mentally strong, that's what you do . . . you carry yourself with grace, pride, and a little bit of "Take that!" like the true G.O.A.T. you are.

MANTRA #4

Life is like a roller coaster. Ride the highs. Endure the lows. There's a lesson in them both.

ROLLER COASTER TIME LINE
PART II

2001 Serena's WTA ranking drops to tenth place, but climbs back to number six going into 2002.

2001 At the US Open in September, Venus and Serena make history as the first sisters to reach the finals of a Grand Slam tournament since the Watson sisters (Maud and Lillian) in 1884. This is also the first time two African American women face each other for the win. Venus defeats Serena 6–2, 6–4.

2002 Serena defeats Capriati at the Italian Open in May, raising her WTA rank to #3.

2001 In August, Serena defeats Capriati in Toronto, in a three-set final.

2002 Serena makes history at the Miami Masters in March by becoming the first player to defeat three high-ranked players in one tournament: Martina Hingis, Venus Williams, and Jennifer Capriati.

2002 In Sydney, Serena sprains her ankle in the first set of her final against Meghann Shaughnessy. Serena withdraws from the Australian Open.

2001 At the French Open, in June, Capriati wins in 3 sets over Serena in the quarterfinals.

2002 In late February–early March, at the State Farm Women's Classic, Serena defeats first Martina Hingis and then Jennifer Capriati in three set matches, marking her first WTA singles title of the year.

2002 Serena lands her third Grand Slam singles title at the US Open in September!

2003 Serena spends the earlier part of the year ranked #1. At the Australian Open, she wins her fourth Grand Slam singles title!

2003 Serena defeats Venus for a fifth straight major at Wimbledon in July. This is Serena's last game of the season, ending with a record of 38 wins, 3 losses.

2002 In July, Serena defeats Venus at Wimbledon and is ranked #1 in the world. This ranking dethrones Venus from the top spot and Serena becomes the third African American woman to earn a #1 ranking.

2003 A knee injury and a quadriceps tendon injury keep her sidelined for two months. Her rank drops to #3.

2003 In August, Serena has surgery to repair her left quadriceps tendon. During recovery, Serena spends time in physical rehabilitation and pursues an interest in acting.

2002 At the French Open, Serena faces her toughest rival for the fourth time: Venus, who is now ranked #2 in the world. Serena outplays Venus, with a final score of 7–5, 6–3, serving up Grand Slam title number two!

2002 Richard and Oracene separate and file for divorce, in October.

2003 Serena's oldest sister, Yetunde Price, is caught in the crossfire of a gang shooting in Compton, in September, not far from the courts Serena and Venus played on.

Serena with her sister, Yetunde Price, at the 2003 ESPY Awards where she won both Best Female Tennis Player and Best Female Athlete

Family, faith, education. In that exact order. Nothing means more to Serena than her family. Her sister Yetunde played a huge role in Serena's life. She was Serena's oldest sister, the one whom Serena trusted with her secrets, her life, and her career. For a brief period, Yetunde even worked for Serena as her personal assistant. If you recall, Serena's move to Florida meant leaving Yetunde behind. For years, she didn't see Yetunde, who, after finishing school, began a life of her own. Yetunde opened a beauty salon and started a family with a son, Jeffrey, a daughter, Justus, and finally another son, Jair. Once Serena began experiencing success—both financially and in the WTA—she purchased an apartment in Los Angeles so she could be close to Yetunde and her niece and nephews when she was in town.

Yetunde's death affected Serena deeply. Not to mention the breakup of her parents' marriage and the injuries suffered that kept her away from the court. Rumors swirled. Maybe Serena wasn't strong enough to pick herself up this time. Could this be the end of her career?

Serena holding the Ladies' Singles trophy at the
2005 Wimbledon Championship

7

SERENA SLAM X 2

On an overcast July day in 2015, it was as if all of London could hear the words: "We love you, Serena!" Scores of fans screamed out as Serena lifted the gold plate, a symbol of Wimbledon victory, to the sky. Dressed in all white, looking like an angel, Serena's face lit up with a mile-wide smile. The applause and cheers were genuine, nothing like what she experienced on that hurtful day at Indian Wells.

All of her hard work prepared her for this moment, where she would waltz off the court, as if floating on a cloud, to attend her press conference. Lights flashed and the crowd went wild as Serena took her seat. For the second time in her career, Serena had won all four major tournaments—the Australian Open, the French Open,

Wimbledon, and the US Open. The first time she did this was between the years 2002 and 2003.

The media called Serena's win the "Serena Slam." You know you're a G.O.A.T. when a record is named after you!

Perhaps more notable than the two Serena Slams are the obstacles that Serena faced to reach this achievement. The racism she and her family faced. The loss of her sister that caused Serena to fall into depression and lose motivation to return to the court. The media's teasing of Serena's body type because it didn't fit their idea of what a female athlete should look like. Still, Serena found the strength to rise above the adversity she faced.

Between Serena's first Serena Slam and her second, a little more than 12 years passed. Somehow, even though she was plagued by injuries and inconsistent rankings during that time, Serena recovered and reclaimed her spot at the top. Call it focus. Call it hard work. We'll just call it a mix of both, sprinkled in with a little bit of G.O.A.T. magic.

At 33 years old, people thought it was time for Serena to hang up her racquet. Because really, what more is there left to do? How many more records are there left to break?

DID YOU KNOW?

If you ask Serena what was the inspiration for powering through her first "Serena Slam," she would say this: rejection. In 2001, at the age of 19, Serena experienced a bad breakup with a boyfriend. With no explanation, he simply stopped calling. This rejection tore her heart to pieces! Instead of allowing the experience to get her down, Serena decided to shift her focus to her goals, her game, her destiny. For Serena, there was a lesson to be learned. Perhaps it is a lesson that everyone can benefit from: In moments of rejection, pick yourself up, and keep pushing until you rediscover your purpose in life. And for Serena, her life was on the court.

The year following Yetunde's death was hard for Serena and her family. Still recovering from previous injuries, Serena routinely went to physical therapy and kept up with her workouts. It was second nature to her to train because that's what she had done six days a week, ever since she was a little girl. But her heart and her mind were not focused on tennis. Venus returned to the court for the Australian Open in January 2004. It would take Serena a little longer to muster the courage to come back, but when she did, she buckled up and faced the future with a mix of fear and fearlessness.

ROLLER COASTER TIME LINE
PART III

2010 Serena falls slightly in her year-end ranking to #4, but increases her win percentage to 86%, up 5% from the previous year, and wins two Grand Slams—the Australian Open and Wimbledon.

2004 Serena loses in the quarterfinals at the French Open, and again at Wimbledon to new tennis phenom, Maria Sharapova. For the first time in years, Serena falls out of the top 10 ranking.

2009 The Associated Press names Serena Female Athlete of the Year, which is well deserved given her record for 2009: She wins five Grand Slam tournaments, two in singles and three in doubles. Serena breaks Justine Henin's record for most prize money earned.

2008 Serena finds her stride, winning her ninth Grand Slam tournament, and finishing the year with a #2 ranking in the world.

2005 Serena begins the season with a win at the Australian Open, beating top-ranked Lindsay Davenport. Shortly after, she suffers more injuries and falls into a deep depression, having not fully recovered from her sister's death. In her final events of the year (Wimbledon; the Internazionali BNL d'Italia in Rome; the US Open; the Rogers Cup in Toronto; and the China Open in Beijing), Serena fails to advance to the quarterfinals. Serena begins seeing a therapist to cope with Yetunde's death.

2006 At the Australian Open, Serena loses in the third round. Her WTA rank drops to #139. More knee injuries mean fewer tournaments. Serena only enters four this year.

2007 Serena reenters the Australian Open, unseeded, ranked #81. The media taunts her for gaining weight, calls her horrible names, and doubts her ability to play well. Facing Maria Sharapova in the finals, Serena crushes her opponent from the first serve. She wins 6–1, 6–2, and wins the Open, silencing the rumors that her career is over.

2015 The hits just keep on coming! Serena finishes the year at #1 for the fifth time, is named *Sports Illustrated* Sportsperson of the Year, becomes the second player since Steffi Graf to hold the top ranking for two consecutive years, and captures her historic second Serena Slam.

2014 Serena hits #1 for the fourth time, holding this ranking for 97 weeks. She wins seven tournament titles and one Grand Slam.

2013 For the third time, Serena ranks #1. She wins 78 singles matches that season, ups her winning percentage to 95% (her highest yet), and picks up two more Grand Slam singles titles.

2016 At 34 years old, Serena wins Wimbledon, making history as the oldest player to win a Grand Slam singles title. She holds the #1 ranking for 186 consecutive weeks, tying Steffi Graf's record, but finishes the year at #2 in the world.

2012 What an historic year for Serena! She jumps up in the ranks, finishing the year at #3, increases her win percentage to 93.55%, and makes history as the second woman to earn the Golden Slam (winning four majors and an Olympic gold).

2011 Serena is diagnosed with a pulmonary embolism, which prevents her from playing the first half of the season. Though her rank falls to #12, her win percentage increases again, this time to 88%.

RIVALS: WHO WOULD WIN?

As you can see, Serena's career has been full of high and low moments. Along the way, she has faced other athletes who could have easily taken her throne. Every athlete wants to be the G.O.A.T. In sports, there's no greater honor. But how can we know who the true G.O.A.T. is without sizing up other players? In tennis, females play for the WTA and males play for the ATP (Association of Tennis Professionals). Therefore, Serena obviously plays other women and not men. But if there can only be *one* G.O.A.T., then maybe we need to compare her skill level against both women and men.

Let's do some fantasy tennis with other contenders and see who would win! Who knows? We just might have this whole G.O.A.T. theory wrong.

Taking a bit of inspiration from the majors, here's how our fantasy tournament will work:

We begin with a draw of all of our participants. To make a good judgment on who would win, we'll look at four key pieces of evidence: Highest Year-End Ranking, Career Titles, Grand Slam Singles Titles, and for good measure, we'll throw in a "Did you know?" category that shows something special enough that might give the contender an edge. As round 1 begins, we will size Serena up to her assigned match. The winner of that round will advance to the second round and will be paired with the next match for round 2. Still analyzing the key evidence, we'll determine a winner for rounds 3 and 4. The competition will stiffen as we advance to the quarterfinals, semifinals, and finals, where the ultimate winner shall be considered the G.O.A.T. Are you ready for a battle of epic proportions? Let's get started.

• • •

ROUND 1
Serena versus Lindsay Davenport

Turning pro in 1993, just two years before Serena, Lindsay Davenport has had her fair share of WTA victories: a 753–194 win-loss ratio, 130 top 10 wins (having defeated Serena and other potential G.O.A.T.s, such as Venus, Jennifer Capriati, and Monica Seles), and a 1996 Olympic gold medal in women's singles. Lindsay's numbers might fall a bit short of Serena's, but there are plenty of reasons why Lindsay should be considered for the G.O.A.T. position, mainly for her work on and *off* the court.

LINDSAY VS SERENA

LINDSAY DAVENPORT

Highest Year-End Ranking:
Lindsay hit #1 a total of four times, in 1998, 2001, 2004, and 2005.

Career Titles: 55

Grand Slam Singles Titles: 3

Did you know?
Lindsay turned pro in 1993 at the age of 16 and by the following year, she cracked the top 10 WTA ranking. Two years after Serena's professional debut, she ranked a very low #304.

SERENA WILLIAMS

Highest Year-End Ranking:
Serena was ranked #1 in the following years: 2002, 2009, 2013, 2014, 2015.

Career Titles: 72

Grand Slam Singles Titles: 23

Did you know?
The win-loss ratio for Serena vs. Lindsay is 10–4.

DECISION: We all know who the winner of round 1 is. Still, Lindsay has made a nice name for herself in tennis, having gone head-to-head with Serena and come out victorious four times. Lindsay has transitioned from pro tennis player to tennis coach to the stars. Who knows, maybe she's grooming the next G.O.A.T. who just might be able to give Serena a run for her money!

ROUND 2
Serena versus Jennifer Capriati

It feels like a natural progression to move on to Jennifer as another of Serena's greatest rivals. You've seen her name pop up several times in this book. Serena and Jennifer have a lot in common. They both started very young, with Serena turning pro at 14 and Jennifer at the even younger age of 13. Both players have suffered hardship in their careers: Serena's injuries and the death of her oldest sister; Jennifer's substance abuse issues and burnout from being thrust in the spotlight at a young age. Both players, however, found an inner strength that allowed them to pick themselves up and return to the court better and stronger. When Jennifer emerged from a hiatus, she really gave Serena some serious competition, particularly in four back-to-back tournaments in the years 2000 and 2001. But what do the overall numbers say? Let's take a look.

JENNIFER VS SERENA

JENNIFER CAPRIATI

Highest Year-End Ranking:
The highest rankings that Jennifer has received was #2 in 2001 and #3 in 2002. When she retired in 2004, her rank was #10.

Career Titles: 14

Grand Slam Singles Titles: 3

Did you know?
Capriati's win-loss record against Serena is 7–10.

SERENA WILLIAMS

Highest Year-End Ranking:
Serena was ranked #1 in the following years: 2002, 2009, 2013, 2014, 2015.

Career Titles: 72

Grand Slam Singles Titles: 23

Did you know?
Serena's toughest tournament against Jennifer took place in the quarterfinals of the 2004 US Open. The umpire made several missed calls that tilted the outcome in Capriati's favor. Television replays later confirmed that the calls should've gone Serena's way. Still, Capriati defeated Serena on her second match point.

DECISION: And the *clear* winner is . . . Serena Williams! When it comes to Grand Slams and career titles, there's really just no comparison.

ROUND 3
Serena versus Maria Sharapova

We're taking a real risk with this pairing. Mainly because if you take a look at the evidence, you might question why Maria Sharapova is a choice to begin with (more on that later). Like any sport, rivalries are inevitable. Rivalries help players raise their game. And in the tennis world, it's no secret that Serena and Maria are true rivals. Any Google search will describe their mutual dislike for each other.

A bit of background is needed here for Maria. Like most tennis pros, she ran the junior circuit first, training in Florida at the Nick Bollettieri Tennis Academy at 9 years old. Early in her professional career, which began at the age of 14, Maria showed a lot of promise—earning majors titles and high rankings in the top 20. Plagued by shoulder injuries and suspension from the WTA for 15 months, Maria returned to international competition in April 2017, poised to knock Serena, the G.O.A.T., off her throne.

MARIA VS SERENA

MARIA SHARAPOVA

Highest Year-End Ranking:
Maria has yet to reach a #1 year-end ranking. Her highest rank, #2, was achieved in 2006, 2012, and 2014.

Career Titles: 36

Grand Slam Singles Titles: 5

Did you know?
Maria made history on August 22, 2005, when she reached #1 in world ranking. As a result, she made history as the first Russian female tennis player to hit the highest WTA ranking.

SERENA WILLIAMS

Highest Year-End Ranking:
Serena was ranked #1 in the following years: 2002, 2009, 2013, 2014, 2015.

Career Titles: 72

Grand Slam Singles Titles: 23

Did you know?
Serena has a win-loss ratio of 19–2 against Maria, making her win percentage 90%.

DECISION: Serena Williams is ahead of Maria Sharapova by leaps and bounds. We've included Maria in this argument for several reasons. First, much like Serena, Maria has shown resilience, particularly when she improved her world rank from #126 to #14 in 2005. In the following year, Maria defeated one of Serena's toughest opponents, Justine Henin, at the US Open. And lastly, Maria has a story with a humble beginning, much like Serena. In 1994, at the age of 7, Maria and her father immigrated to the United States with only $700, no English language skills, and a dream to make it to the pros. On her 14th birthday, April 19, 2001, Maria made her professional debut.

Maria might *still* have a chance at the throne. Maria's rank as of July 2018 is #21, compared to Serena's #28. In the earlier part of 2018, Serena ranked as low as #449, but you'll soon discover the precious reason why. Maria gets an "A" for effort, but Serena the G.O.A.T. moves on to round 4.

ROUND 4
Serena versus Justine Henin

Justine's greatest showdown against Serena occurred in 2007, when she defeated her at three Grand Slams in a row. In the seven times they've met at Grand Slams, Henin led 4–3. Pretty impressive! So it's only natural that we would pit these rivals against each other.

JUSTINE VS SERENA

JUSTINE HENIN

Highest Year-End Ranking:
Justine has ranked #1 a total of
three times in the years 2003,
2006, 2007.

Career Titles: 43

Grand Slam Singles Titles: 7

Did you know?
Justine's career total win
percentage is 82%, not too far
behind Serena's 85.65%.

SERENA WILLIAMS

Highest Year-End Ranking:
Serena was ranked #1 in the
following years: 2002, 2009,
2013, 2014, 2015.

Career Titles: 72

Grand Slam Singles Titles: 23

Did you know?
Serena has played Justine in
14 tournaments, winning 8 and
losing 6.

DECISION: Serena advances to the quarter finals! If Henin were still playing today, she would likely be tough competition for Serena. She retired in 2008 due to burnout, having ended her career with a number one ranking. This left the door wide open for Serena, who is actually a year younger than Henin. Henin returned to tennis briefly, only to retire for good in 2011. By that point, Serena had already won her first Serena Slam and was on her way to winning a second one.

QUARTERFINALS
Serena versus Venus

You had to have seen this coming! Venus is Serena's oldest rival by birthright. They grew up and trained together since their childhood years. Early in both of their careers, Venus had the leg up. She was the media darling, creating early buzz, years ahead of her professional debut. Venus turned pro before Serena and was the first of the sisters to land a major endorsement contract. Venus served Serena serious game in singles matches, but at some point the tides began to shift. The numbers don't lie. Take a look for yourself:

VENUS VS SERENA

VENUS WILLIAMS

Highest Year-End Ranking:
Venus finished the 2002 season ranked #2, though she spent 11 weeks at #1 in the earlier part of the year.

Career Titles: 49

Grand Slam Singles Titles: 7

Did you know?
Venus made history in 1997 when she because the first unseeded women's finalist for the US Open.

SERENA WILLIAMS

Highest Year-End Ranking:
Serena was ranked #1 in the following years: 2002, 2009, 2013, 2014, 2015.

Career Titles: 72

Grand Slam Singles Titles: 23

Did you know?
At just 17 years old, Serena became the first African American woman to win a Grand Slam title since Althea Gibson.

DECISION: All siblings battle it out once in a while. Serena and Venus are no different. When they do play against each other, fans and media alike describe their matches as tentative and disappointing. Much of this has to do with their upbringing and the strong bond they have as sisters. Richard simply was against his girls competing against each other. When it no longer became avoidable, Venus dominated Serena in the earlier part of their careers. That shifted in 1999, however. Serena currently holds a win-loss ratio of 17–12. It looks like Venus has some catching up to do.

SEMIFINALS
Serena versus Monica Seles

We've mentioned Steffi Graf's name a few times in this book as a potential G.O.A.T. Between the years of 1988 and 1990, she won eight Grand Slam singles tournaments. But then newcomer Monica Seles stepped onto the scene and dethroned the high-ranking tennis princess. So, it's only right that we include Monica Seles as a real contender. From 1990 to 1993, Seles won 8 majors, putting an end to Graf's dominance. Seles claimed the #1 rank in 1991, 1992, and then again in 1995. Then the unthinkable happened. During a 1993 tournament in

Hamburg, Germany, a crazed Steffi Graf fan stabbed Monica in the back, narrowly missing her spinal cord. The fan claimed that he hurt Monica so that Steffi Graf could return to her rightful ranking. Sadly, while Graf played no role in this act of violence, this is exactly what happened. During Monica's recovery, Graf would go on to win 6 more Grand Slams. Seles returned to tennis in 1995, where she would claim one more Grand Slam, bringing her total to 9, but she would never fully recover from the attack. Seles officially retired in 2008.

MONICA VS SERENA

MONICA SELES

Highest Year-End Ranking:
Monica ranked #1 in 1991, 1992, and 1995.

Career Titles: 53

Grand Slam Singles Titles: 9

Did you know?
Monica's win-loss ratio is 1–4 against Serena. She defeated Serena only once, in 2001 at the Estyle.com Classic.

SERENA WILLIAMS

Highest Year-End Ranking:
Serena was ranked #1 in the following years: 2002, 2009, 2013, 2014, 2015.

Career Titles: 72

Grand Slam Singles Titles: 23

Did you know?
Having watched Seles's rise to tennis stardom, Serena has credited Seles as an inspiration for her career.

DECISION: Monica Seles's career is an unfortunate fairy tale–turned–nightmare story. At her peak, Seles would've given Serena a real fight. She was well on her way to defeating the G.O.A.T. of the 1980s and 1990s. Unfortunately, that frightful day in Hamburg changed the course of her career. Therefore, it is with a bit of sadness and a lot of respect that we give this win to Serena Williams, who moves on to a bonus round.

BONUS ROUND
Serena versus Roger Federer

There's something pretty awesome about this pairing, mainly because of the marked differences between men and women's tennis. For starters, men play five sets versus women's three sets. This fact might lead people to think that men play longer because they have more stamina. That simply isn't true. Women have played five-set matches, particularly between the years of 1984 to 1998 during the finals of the WTA Championships in New York. By 1999, the tournament switched to a three-set format. Another slight difference between men and women's tennis is that depending on the surface, men and women play with different types of balls. On hard courts, women play with a "regular duty" ball, which is lighter and livelier, while men use an "extra duty" ball, which is heavier. On clay courts, however, the extra duty ball is fair game for both men and women. If we are to truly decide who the G.O.A.T. is, it shouldn't have to be defined by gender. Men and women put in the same effort, endure same training, and equally have the potential to come out on top. In men's tennis, it doesn't get any better than Roger Federer. The same can be said about Serena for women's tennis. When it all boils down to it, a win is a win.

ROGER VS SERENA

ROGER FEDERER

Highest Year-End Ranking:
Roger was ranked #1 in men's
tennis in the following years:
2004–2007 and 2009.

Career Titles: 98

Grand Slam Singles Titles: 20

Did you know?
Roger's record wins for playing the
top 10 in the Open Era is 214,
compared to Serena's 172.

SERENA WILLIAMS

Highest Year-End Ranking:
Serena was ranked #1 in the
following years: 2002, 2009,
2013, 2014, 2015.

Career Titles: 72

Grand Slam Singles Titles: 23

Did you know?
With 23 Grand Slams under her
belt, Serena is one slam away from
reaching Margaret Court's record.
The most impressive part is that
her Grand Slam record is higher
than all of the men's leading Grand
Slam title winners. ALL 28 of them!

HISTORY OF TENNIS

What era is the Open Era referring to, exactly? To understand this, it's important to know the difference between amateur and professional tennis. Though amateurs can be as competitive as professionals, the main difference is that amateurs are not paid for their participation in sporting events, unlike professionals who are. Beginning in 1877, Wimbledon, the world's oldest and original Grand Slam event, featured amateurs only. The world's top professional players did not compete because they needed to make a living. So these players competed in such tournaments as the French Pro Championships and the US Pro Tennis Championships. As a result, prior to 1968, the Grand Slam tournaments did not draw top talent, which led to minimal public interest and financial gain. This was bad for the sport! That changed in 1968 when professional players qualified for major tournaments with guaranteed prize money. The quality of tennis improved drastically and resulted in greater interest from the public and sponsors who paid to cover and advertise the events. The Open Era thus refers to the time in tennis after 1968.

DECISION: Okay, okay. We know what you're thinking. *Just look at Roger's career titles! And my goodness, check out his top 10 wins!* Roger and Serena certainly tie for year-end rankings. Each have ranked #1 for five years. Another important fact to mention is their Olympic performances in singles matches. Roger has won one gold (doubles) and one silver (singles) medal, whereas Serena has earned a total of four gold medals (3 doubles, 1 single). This tips the scales a bit in her favor. The real stand-out fact is her Grand Slam record. Aside from Margaret Court's total of 24, Serena has wiped out the competition on both the women and men's side. If that's not G.O.A.T. level, we don't know what is! Therefore, the winner of this battle is Serena Williams! She advances to the finals, where she will face her toughest competition yet.

FINALS
Serena versus Steffi Graf

This final pairing shouldn't be a surprise. After all, Serena has chased Steffi's records for years and it appears she's well on her way to surpassing her. Or . . . maybe not? Steffi Graf is a tennis legend. If anything, Steffi's accomplishments have raised the bar for players like Serena Williams. Has Serena done enough to tip the scales in her favor? Let's take a look.

STEFFI VS SERENA

STEFFI GRAF

Highest Year-End Ranking:
Steffi has held the WTA's highest ranking for four consecutive years, twice. She was #1 between the years of 1987 and 1990, and then again from 1993–1996.

Career Titles: 107

Grand Slam Singles Titles: 22

Did you know?
Steffi spent a whopping 377 weeks ranked at #1. As of 2017, Serena's total was 319 weeks. Given that Serena is still playing and Steffi has long since retired, Serena might be able to surpass Steffi's record.

SERENA WILLIAMS

Highest Year-End Ranking:
Serena was ranked #1 in the following years: 2002, 2009, 2013, 2014, 2015.

Career Titles: 72

Grand Slam Singles Titles: 23

Did you know?
Serena and Steffi have only played each other twice. At 29 years old, Steffi defeated a young Serena at Sydney in January 1999. Serena returned the favor a few months later at Indian Wells.

VERDICT

This one might be a toss-up! In tennis circles, the Grand Slam is the crown jewel, the highest goal to be achieved. If we're judging by this alone, Serena has Steffi beat. Serena has 23 Grand Slams, compared to Steffi's 22. And as of 2018, Serena is *still* playing! Who knows if she has more Grand Slams to come? On the other hand, there's a lot to be said about Steffi's numbers. She has 35 more career singles titles than Serena and outranks her in weeks spent at #1. Also, Steffi has completed a Grand Slam by winning all four majors *within a single calendar year*. Not even Serena has been able to do that . . . *yet*. In the end, we'll need to get really nitpicky here to choose the winner. So let's bring in some other determining factors, beginning with the Olympics. Serena edges out Graf in medal count, with four golds to Graf's one. Granted, Serena's gold medals are a result of three doubles and one single, which you could say equals Graf's count, but we have to consider that Serena has never finished in second or third place. Graf earned a bronze at the 1988 Summer Olympics in Seoul, Korea and a silver at the 1992 Olympics in Barcelona, Spain. We also have to take popular opinion into account. Serena has won the Associated Press's Female Athlete of the Year three times (2009, 2013, 2015). Steffi Graf has won only once in 1989. Serena was also named *Sports Illustrated*'s Sportsperson of the Year, an honor that Graf cannot add to her résumé. That said, we'll go ahead and call it: game, set, match! It was a tough battle, but the crown still goes to Serena Williams!

9

WHO'D WE MISS?

Is Serena your choice for the G.O.A.T.? She certainly has the skills, the drive, and a host of records to prove it. Lots of tennis players have also earned titles and medals, and have made history. The pros mentioned in the previous chapter show some real contenders. With the exception of Roger Federer, all have played against Serena at some point in their career. And if they were formidable enough, they even celebrated some victories. But G.O.A.T doesn't stand for the Greatest Of Right Now—it stands for the Greatest Of *All Time*, which means that we should also consider the greats who have come *before* Serena. Some are living legends! Perhaps some of the choices listed in this chapter should wear the crown. After all, they paved the path for greatness, which, again, is not always defined by statistics and records. Years before Serena even set foot on the professional court, these potential G.O.A.T.s were making waves on and off the court.

BILLIE JEAN KING (1943–)

Billie Jean King was the type of player who carried the weight of women's tennis world on her shoulders—literally. Records aside (and we'll get to that in a moment), players like Serena Williams owe a huge debt of gratitude to King for her contributions to the sport. In King's time of playing tennis, men and women did not receive equal pay. In 1971, King became the first female athlete to earn more than $100,000, but this was still less than the potential earnings in men's tennis. In fact, when she won the US Open in 1972, she earned $15,000 less than Ilie Năstase, the men's champion. King made a powerful statement by refusing to play the US Open the following year and finally, in 1973, the US Open became the first major tournament to give equal prize money to both men and women. King went on to found the Women's Tennis Association in 1973 to ensure equality for female tennis players. For her efforts off the court, President Barack

Obama awarded King the Presidential Medal of Freedom, the nation's highest civilian honor, in 2009.

Serena can certainly thank Billie Jean King for those extra zeroes in her paycheck, but what about Billie Jean King's other records? King has been ranked #1 in the world six times (1966–1968, 1971–1972, 1974) and #1 in the United States seven times (1965–1967, 1970–1973). She has 12 Grand Slam singles titles and 129 career singles titles. Serena has more Grand Slams, for sure, but it looks like she has some catching up to do on the career titles—57 more to be exact! Without a doubt, Billie Jean King deserves to be added to the G.O.A.T. conversation.

MARGARET COURT (1942–)

Margaret has so many accolades in tennis, it's hard not to think of her as a potential G.O.A.T. Make no mistake, she was the most dominant female tennis player during the 1960s and 1970s. For starters, she won 24 Grand Slam singles titles. With Serena's record of 23, it's likely that Serena can surpass Court's record given that she is *still* playing tennis. Court also boasts 194 career singles titles, was inducted into the Tennis Hall of Fame, and enjoyed an injury-free career. These were all things that any tennis player could wish for.

Does that mean that Margaret Court is the real G.O.A.T.? Maybe . . . but maybe *not*. Consider this: During Court's golden years of tennis, her biggest competition were players such as Ann Jones (7 Grand Slams), Françoise Dürr (1 Grand Slam), and Billie Jean King (12 Grand Slams).

In other words, Margaret Court never had the chance to face the likes of Serena. Given the lower caliber of competition in 1960s and 1970s, we can't say with certainty that Margaret Court would be a G.O.A.T. by today's standards.

CHRIS EVERT (1954–)

Chris Evert is an underrated choice for G.O.A.T., mainly because of her icy demeanor on the court. There's a reason why fans dubbed her the "Ice Maiden." Evert didn't play tournaments to make friends. She had one thing in mind . . . winning. This is something Serena can definitely identify with! And Evert had the goods to show for it: 154 career singles titles, #1 ranking seven times (1974–1978, 1980–1981), she never even fell out of the Top 10, having retired at #10 in 1989, and 18 Grand Slam singles titles to her name.

Is this enough to substantiate her G.O.A.T.-ness? She trails Serena in Grand Slam singles titles. And while she competed in the 1988 Seoul Olympics, she did not get a medal. Serena, on the other hand, is a four-time Olympian (Sydney, 2000; Beijing, 2008; London, 2012; and Rio de Janeiro, 2016). Aside from these facts, we should consider her performance alongside her peers of the 1970s and 1980s. Billie Jean King and Margaret Court defeated Evert at the 1973 French Open and Wimbledon, respectively. Czech pro Martina Navratilova chased Evert in 10 Grand Slam singles finals, in the 1983/1984 Year-End Championship finals, and at the Australian Open in 1988 where Navratilova outplayed her in the doubles tournament with Pam Shriver. If Evert was unable to overpower three other potential G.O.A.T.'s, we're not sure how she would measure up against Serena.

MARTINA NAVRATILOVA (1956–)

We could have included Martina Navratilova in the previous chapter, given that she's played against Serena. However, we factored in that she was on her way to retirement just as Serena turned pro. As a result, we'll include her here. Judging by Navratilova's wins against Chris Evert, she has to be in the running! Like Evert, Navratilova holds some impressive stats: 18 Grand Slam singles titles, 168 career titles in the Open Era (and still holds this record!), and #1 ranking six times (1979, 1982–1986). She is known for her aggressive style of play, which contributed to her court dominance from the mid-1970s to the 1990s.

Off the court, Navratilova should be commended for her contributions to society, mainly for her activism for animal and gay rights. She even earned the National Equality Award from the Human Rights Campaign, in 2000. If that's not G.O.A.T.-level recognition, we don't know what more to say!

But if we were to pit her against Serena, who would come out victorious?

The tennis of Navratilova's years was certainly different than Serena's current style of play. Navratilova was a serve-and-volley player, a technique that's pretty much extinct in today's tennis. In this style, after hitting a serve, the player moves to the net to hit the volley (striking the ball without letting it bounce). The main reason this style is no longer popular is that the advancements in racquets and strings no longer call for it. If Navratilova were to serve-and-volley Serena today, it's likely Serena would return a swift, missile-like hit, clocking in at 195 kmph (almost 122 mph), a feat she accomplished in Australia in 2017. Could Navratilova handle that? She tried, actually, coming out of retirement for a brief time, to team up with Russian pro, Svetlana Kuznetsova, and face both Venus and Serena in the Australian Open in 2003. The match lasted barely an hour, with the Williams sisters crushing their opponents, 6–2, 6–3. Need we say more?

ARTHUR ASHE (1943–1993)

We couldn't let this chapter slide without including a male player. Since we're discussing historical, groundbreaking pioneers, it's only fitting that we mention Arthur Ashe. We'll begin with the stats: 3 Singles Grand Slams, 51 career titles, a 75.3% win record, and a #1 world rank in 1968. We know what you're thinking. These numbers don't surpass Serena's. Accurate! Sometimes being considered a G.O.A.T. goes beyond statistics. In Ashe's case, the impact that he had on tennis allowed Serena to become the player that she is today.

During his short career, he made a host of firsts: He was the first African American selected for the United

States Davis Cup Team, the first African American ranked as the world's #1, the first African American winner of the United States Amateur Championship, and the first African American to win Wimbledon. Ashe also served in the United States Army for two years, which is quite the G.O.A.T. move! Arthur Ashe was more than a tennis player. He was an activist, who used his celebrity status to speak out against apartheid in South Africa. Apartheid is the act of separating people based on their race. Ashe passed away at the young age of 49, but was awarded the Presidential Medal of Freedom in June 1993, four months after his death. In 1997, the Arthur Ashe Stadium was constructed in Queens, New York, as the home of the US Open. The man has an entire stadium named after him! Sure, Serena has the numbers, but does she represent all the diverse ways one can be considered the G.O.A.T?

Making the case for the Greatest of All Time is not easy. We've taken a close look at some serious contenders in this debate, but maybe we haven't included one of your favorites. Who else deserves to be a part of this conversation? One thing is for sure: With so many different variables to consider, it's almost impossible for everyone to agree on the one true G.O.A.T. But it's definitely fun to make the case!

MANTRA #5

Your destiny is shaped by the people around you. Be kind to them. Love them. Remember them. Work hard for them. Work hard for... you.

Serena opens the Serena Williams
Secondary School in Matooni, Kenya.

10

OFF THE COURT

In the previous chapter, we focused on the goodwill of other potential G.O.A.T.s, such as Arthur Ashe and Billie Jean King. Their work off the court certainly has played a huge role in defining them as legends. But has Serena done something to match the standards they have set? Actually, she's done a lot.

Three years after Yetunde's death, a goodwill trip came at the perfect time to help Serena heal from depression. Her destination? Africa. A gold mine of culture and a real opportunity to connect with her roots. In November 2006, Serena traveled to Ghana and Senegal with her mother and sisters Isha and Lyndrea, followed by a 2008 visit to South Africa and Kenya. Initially, Serena viewed the trip as a way to bring real meaning to the stories she had heard about her ancestors—the continent from which they came, the reality of being sold as slaves, the endurance through hardship in America. But what she got out of it was so much more.

Serena toured the countries, visiting schools and giving free tennis lessons to children. Beyond the poverty and hardship, Serena could see the light in these children's eyes. They had a real love for tennis! They weren't fortunate enough to have the latest tennis equipment, yet with the little they had, they showed strength and raw talent. The courts were cracked and run-down, a startling reminder to Serena of where she came from, how far she had come, and how much there was left to do.

In addition to giving tennis lessons to these children, Serena and her family volunteered for the United Nations International Children's Emergency Fund (UNICEF). UNICEF provides assistance to children and mothers in impoverished countries. Many of the villages Serena visited were poor and did not have access to proper medical care. Serena and her family visited these villages, hospitals, and clinics to distribute vitamins, polio vaccines, medicines, and bed nets to prevent the spread of malaria.

The 2006 trip left Serena deeply affected by the resilience of the African people. Even in bad conditions, they found a way to be hopeful. The experience redefined

Serena's purpose in life on the court and especially off the court. When she returned to Africa in 2008, she was determined to go beyond all that she had done the first time around. In Senegal, the cost to educate a child is 10 cents a day. Many parents could not afford that because their earnings were already so low. Given her wealth, Serena realized that the best investment she could make would be to contribute to the future of African children.

Serena met with Abdoulaye Wade, the president of Senegal, and offered to build a school students could attend for free. She didn't stop there. Working alongside a group called Build African Schools and technology company Hewlett-Packard (HP), Serena donated $60,000 to construct a school in Kenya. With her contribution, a school was built with plumbing and solar-powered panels and outfitted with the best HP technology. This project also helped pay local construction workers a livable wage.

On November 14, 2008, Serena stood before the blue ribbon that blocked the entrance to the new school, aptly named the Serena Williams Secondary School. As she cut the ribbon, an overwhelming feeling of pride washed over her. That moment was better than any Grand Slam, any Olympic medal, any record that she had broken. The children who would go on to attend this school would have a real chance of success. Serena knew this because of the values that her parents taught her growing up— that education is the key to everything. Serena could have easily written a $60,000 check and gone on with her life. But instead she chose to dig her hands in the African soil, help the village build their future, and be there to witness it in its completion. Serena would go on to develop her own charity, the Serena Williams Fund, and build more schools in Uganda and Jamaica, years later. For Serena, these experiences were the greatest of all time.

DID YOU KNOW?

In addition to Serena's charitable contributions, Serena has done some fun things off the court. Bitten by the acting bug, Serena has appeared on such television shows as: The Simpsons, My Wife and Kids, The Game, and Drop Dead Diva.

Serena has always turned heads. From hair beads to biker outfits, the media loves to highlight her ever-changing fashions. It's no surprise that she tried her hand at designing. Briefly attending the Art Institute of Fort Lauderdale, Serena used her knowledge to design for Nike, start her own fashion line, Aneres (Serena spelled backward), and create a signature line for the Home Shopping Network (HSN) and Walmart.

11

WHAT THE FUTURE HOLDS

If Serena Williams were to end her career today, there would be plenty to say to defend the idea that she is the greatest tennis player of all time. With 23 Grand Slams, she is poised to surpass Margaret Court's record of 24. At the age of 35, she was and still is the only player—male or female—to win this amount in the **Open Era**. In the tennis world, this is the stuff that legends are made of.

As of 2018, Serena is not the player, nor the person, she was when she first stepped onto the professional court in Quebec City. She is older, wiser, stronger. And what's even sweeter is that Serena Williams can add a new role to her extensive résumé—mom.

Serena met Alexis Ohanian in May 2015 and they

Serena along with her husband Alexis Ohanian and their daughter Alexis Olympia watch a match at the 2018 Fed Cup in Asheville, NC.

began dating a month later. The two could not be any more different: Alexis is a self-confessed computer geek (and cofounder of the popular website, Reddit). Serena is an athlete and definitely not a tech-geek. Alexis is German-Armenian. Serena is African American. But for Alexis and Serena, their differences are what drew them to each other.

In January 2017, Serena defeated her sister Venus at the Australian Open, making it her 23rd Grand Slam singles title. Three months later, she posted a picture of her stomach with the hashtag #20weeks. She quickly deleted the photo, but it was too late. The secret was out. Scores of fans did the math and realized that Serena must have won the Australian Open while she was pregnant. Two days before the tournament, Serena learned that she and Alexis were expecting a child. Nervous about playing while pregnant, she consulted with her doctors, who assured her that it was safe. When Serena defeated Venus, the older sister jokingly said, months later, that the match was unfair from the start because it was two against one.

When Serena left the WTA Tour to give birth, she was ranked #1. On September 1, 2017 Serena and Alexis welcomed their daughter, Alexis Olympia Ohanian Jr. Shortly after, Serena took to social media to give fans a fun fact behind Alexis's initials, AO, to commemorate the Australian Open that they won *together*.

ALL ABOUT WTA RANKINGS

In the WTA, ranks are not a result of one major win. Ranks are determined by the players' results over the course of 52 weeks, which should include a maximum of 16 singles and 11 doubles. The tournaments included are: Grand Slams, WTA Finals, Premier Mandatory, and Premier 5 tournaments. Summer Olympics results used to contribute to rankings, but that practice was discontinued in 2016.

As a result of the ranking system, Serena's #1 rank fell because she did not play any tournaments after the Australian Open in 2017—because she was pregnant. Serena is currently working her way back up the rankings, which isn't a new obstacle for her.

After 14 months away from the court, Serena set her sights on her first major tournament since giving birth—the 2018 French Open. Her return to tennis was overshadowed by a low ranking of #453, a rank that dropped dramatically during her maternity leave. This meant that Serena had to face tough competition early on. Serena defeated three opponents before ultimately withdrawing from the tournament due to a pectoral injury that hampered her serves. This happened just before she was supposed to play Maria Sharapova. Despite this disappointment, the roller-coaster time line of Serena's career shows how often Serena has risen above every challenge that comes her way, and something tells us she's not done yet.

In her autobiography *On the Line*, Serena recalls the one question the media often asks her: *At the end of your career, how would you like to be remembered?* This is a tough question for anyone to answer. Maybe Serena wants to be remembered for her big heart, or maybe she wants to be remembered as someone who is well-rounded, since she has found success in many different areas of life. But one thing is for certain. The world will always think of Serena Jameka Williams-Ohanian as one of the most talented, hardworking, toughest, and greatest tennis players of all time.

GLOSSARY

ACE: a winning shot where the opponent is unable to hit the ball

BACKHAND: when a player positions the racket behind the body for a backswing

DROPSHOT: a shot where the ball bounces low and near the net, making it difficult for the opponent to reach

FOREHAND: when a player positions the racket across the body, toward the desired direction for the shot

GRAND SLAM: There are four **majors** in tennis, also known as Grand Slams: The Australian Open, the French Open, Wimbledon, and the US Open. A player who wins all four in the same calendar year becomes a Grand Slam champion. Though not covered in the book, there are other categories of Slams as well:

- Non-Calendar Year Grand Slam—winning four majors, though not in the same calendar year

- Career Grand Slam—winning all four majors at any point in the player's career

- Golden Slam—winning all four majors, plus an Olympic gold

OLYMPICS: originating in Greece over 3,000 years ago, the Olympics consist of various athletic competitions featuring contestants from many nations, held every four years.

OPEN ERA: a period in tennis, beginning in 1968, where top professional players were allowed to compete in Grand Slam tournaments

SEEDING: a system used to make sure top-ranked players don't meet in early rounds of a tournament

SERVE: the starting shot in tennis where a player throws the ball in the air and hits it with a racket

UNSEEDED: A player who has not been seeded (or highly ranked) among the Top 16

USTA: (United States Tennis Association) A professional league, made up of rules and regulations for tennis players to follow

VOLLEY: when a player hits the ball before it touches the ground

WTA: (Women's Tennis Association): the main organizational body for professional's women's tennis

BIBLIOGRAPHY

"Althea Gibson." *Biography.com*, A&E Networks Television. February 27, 2018.www.biography.com/people/althea-gibson-9310580.

"Australian Open 2018: Venus Williams, Sloane Stephens upset, Rafael Nadal rolls." *CBS Sports*. January 15, 2018. Accessed June 1, 2018. https://www.cbssports.com/tennis/news/australian-open-2018-venus-williams-sloane-stephens-upset-rafael-nadal-rolls/.

Bieler, Des. "Serena Williams says she was 'nervous' to play in Australian Open while pregnant." *The Washington Post*. April 26, 2017. Accessed May 30, 2018. https://www.washingtonpost.com/news/early-lead/wp/2017/04/26/serena-williams-says-she-was-nervous-to-play-in-australian-open-while-pregnant/?utm_term=.8b5370a3c5f2.

Being Serena. HBO Sports, May 4, 2018.

Benammar, Emily. "Martina Navratilova says 'sexist' view to training means the serve is undervalued in women's tennis." January 27, 2017. Accessed May 3, 2018. http://www.heraldsun.com.au/sport/tennis/martina-navratilova-says-sexist-view-to-trainingmeansthe-serve-is-undervalued-inwomenstennis/newsstory/69f32e0070a1b8363554a2d8f5a65d75.

Buckley Jr., James. *Who are Venus and Serena Williams?*, New York: Penguin Workshop, 2017.

Chase, Curtis. "This is Serena Williams' last week at No. 1. Will she ever get back?" Fox Sports. May 8, 2017. Accessed May 30, 2018. https://www.foxsports.com/tennis/gallery/serena-williams-pregnant-wta-ranking-1-goat-best-tennis-player-ever-comeback-050817.

Chase, Chris. "Was 2013 the best year of Serena Williams' magnificent career?" *USA Today Sports.* October 28, 2013. Accessed May 10, 2018. https://ftw.usatoday.com/2013/10/serena-williams-2013-wta-championships-best-year-career.

Chase, Chris. "Was Serena Williams' 2014 a success or disappointment?" *USA Today Sports.* October 26, 2014. Accessed May 12, 2018. https://ftw.usatoday.com/2014/10/serena-williams-2014-wta-finals-success-disappoitnment

Chowdhury, Saj. "French Open: Serena Williams says her black catsuit made her feel like a superhero." *BBC Sport.* May 29, 2018. Accessed June 1, 2018. https://www.bbc.com/sport/tennis/44294118.

Christopher, Matt. *Serena Williams: Legends in Sports. New York: Little, Brown, 2017.*

Clarke, Liz. "Serena Williams completes Golden Slam with demolition of Maria Sharapova." *The Washington Post.* August 4, 2012. Accessed June 1, 2018. https://www.washingtonpost.com/sports/olympics/serena-williams-completes-golden-slam-with-demolition-of-maria-sharapova/2012/08/04/c04d3288-de70-11e1-8e43-4a3c4375504a_story.html?utm_term=.fb8815d8abb8.

Coutinho, Austin. "Maria Sharapova-Serena Williams to Graf vs Seles: Why women's tennis needs great rivalries." *FirstPost.* September 16, 2017. Accessed June 3, 2018. https://www.firstpost.com/sports/maria-sharapova-serena-williams-to-graf-vs-seles-why-womens-tennis-needs-great-rivalries-4049413.html.

Curtis, Jake. "Ranking the 10 Best Rivalries in Tennis History." *Bleacher Report.* Accessed May 5, 2018. http://bleacherreport.com/articles/1703668-ranking-the-10-best-rivalries-in-tennis-history/.

De Giulio, Bill. "Top 10 Greatest Women's Tennis Players of All Time."
How They Play. September 10, 2018. Accessed October 1, 2018.
https://howtheyplay.com/individual-sports/Top-10-Greatest-Female-
Tennis-Players-of-All-Time.

Dickson, Mike. "Jennifer Capriati at 40: from the golden girl of tennis to
a life battling drugs and injuries . . . what happened to the American?"
Daily Mail. March 26, 2016. Accessed May 3, 2018.
http://www.dailymail.co.uk/sport/tennis/article-3511736/Jennifer-Capriati-40-
America-s-one-time-golden-girl-virtual-recluse-injuries-drugs-took-toll.html.

Finn, Robin. "Tennis; A Family Tradition at Age 14." *The New York Times.*
October 31, 1995. Accessed May 19, 2018.
https://www.nytimes.com/1995/10/31/sports/tennis-a-family-
tradition-at-age-14.html.

Finn, Robin. "Teen-ager Fighting to Turn at 14, Puts off Lawsuit for
Now." *The New York Times.* October 6, 1995. Accessed May 4, 2018.
https://www.nytimes.com/1995/10/06/sports/tennis-teen-ager-
fighting-to-turn-pro-at-14-puts-off-lawsuit-for-now.html.

Geoffreys, Clayton. *Serena Williams: The Inspiring Story of One of Tennis'
Greatest Legends.* South Carolina, 2017.

Isaacson, Melissa. "Whatever Happened to The First Person To Beat Serena
Williams?" *Espn.com.* January 15, 2015. Accessed May 12, 2018.
http://www.espn.com/espnw/news-commentary/article/12167370/what-
ever-happened-first-person to beat-serena-williams.

Jones, Ellen and Robert Myers. "Is Serena Williams the Greatest Female
Tennis Player of All Time?" July 10, 2015. Accessed May 5, 2018.
http://theconversation.com/is-serena-williams-the-greatest-female-
tennis-player-of-all-time-44527.

Kanter, Sharon. "Serena Williams Teases New Namesake Fashion Line At
Her Documentary Series Premiere." *People.com.* April 26, 2018. Accessed
May 10, 2018.
https://people.com/style/serena-williams-fashion-line-debut-documentary/.

Keber, Ashley, Thomas Livengood, Carol L. Otis, Kathleen Stroia, and Sarka
Vitkova. "WTA Age Eligibility Rule and Player Development Programmes."
Accessed May 6, 2018.
http://www.aspetar.com/journal/viewarticle.aspx?id=188#.
WvEHhmNlneQ.

Lewis, Femi. "5 Outstanding Black Women Tennis Champs." ThoughtCo. June
28, 2017. Accessed June 1, 2018.
https://www.thoughtco.com/top-african-american-women-in-
tennis-45324.

"Maria Sharapova." *Biography.com,* A&E Networks Television, July 9,
2018, www.biography.com/people/maria-sharapova-13790853.

Mohamed, Ashfak. "Who's better—Steffi or Serena?" *Iol.co.za.* January 30,
2017. Accessed June 2, 2018.
https://www.iol.co.za/sport/opinion/whos-better-steffi-or-serena-7560725.

"Most Tennis Grand Slam Titles Winners (Men & Women)."
Total Sportstek. September 10, 2018. Accessed September 11, 2018.
https://www.totalsportek.com/tennis/grand-slam-titles-winners-mens-
women/.

"Navratilova, Martina." *Encyclopedia.com.* The Gale Group.
Accessed June 2, 2018.
https://www.encyclopedia.com/people/sports-and-games/sports-
biographies/martina-navratilova.

Newman, Elizabeth. "No room for Body Image Criticism in Serena
Williams' Grand Slam Chase." *Sports Illustrated.* July 14, 2015.
Accessed June 1, 2018.
https://www.si.com/tennis/2015/07/14/serena-williams-body-image-
wta-tennis.

Quintanilla, Blanca M. "Stabbed Monica Seles Attacked Steffi
fan." *New York Daily News.* May 1, 1993. Accessed May 2, 2018.
http://www.nydailynews.com/sports/more-sports/stabbed-monica-
seles-attacked-steffi-fan-article 1.2097990.

BIBLIOGRAPHY

"Serena Williams: All the achievements from a remarkable career."
USA Today Sports. August 9, 2016. Accessed June 4, 2018.
https://www.usatoday.com/story/sports/olympics/rio-
2016/2016/08/09/serena-williams-olympics-grand-slam/88442570/.

Slater, Jim. "Steffi Graf and Monica Seles had big influence on my career—
Serena Williams." *Sports 360.* February 5, 2015. Accessed May 5, 2018.
http://sport360.com/article/tennis/international-tennis/41662/steffi-graf-
and-monica-seles-had-big-influence-my-career-serena-williams.

Tandon, Kamakshi. "The Woman Who Had The Nerve To Beat Serena At 3
Straight Majors." *Espn.com.* September 5, 2015. Accessed May10, 2018.
http://www.espn.com/espnw/news-commentary/article/13588155/the-
woman-had-nerve-beatserena-3-straight-majors.

Tignor, Steve. "1993: Monica Seles' Stabbing." *Tennis.com.* September 24,
2015. Accessed May10, 2018.
http://www.tennis.com/pro-game/2015/09/1993-stopping-unstoppable-
monica-selesstabbing/55433/.

Tignor, Steve. "2004: Mariana Alves' Missed Call Ushers in Hawk-Eye."
Tennis.com. November 19, 2015. Accessed May 10, 2018.
http://www.tennis.com/pro-game/2015/11/2004-mariana-alves-missed-
call-ushers-hawk-eye/56853/.

Trollope, Matt. "Part III: Men and Women's Tennis Compared." *Tennis Mash.*
April 27, 2017. Accessed May 11, 2018.
https://tennismash.com/2017/04/27/part-iii-mens-womens-tennis-
compared/.

"Williams completes historic 'Serena Slam'." *Wimbledon News.* July 11,
2015. Accessed June1, 2018.
https://www.wimbledon.com/en_GB/news/articles/2015-07-11/serena_
slam_completed_with_sixth_wimbledon_title.html.

The Williams Sisters: E! True Hollywood Story. E! Network, 2004.

Williams, Serena, and Paisner, Daniel. *On the Line.* New York: Grand Central
Publishing, 2009.

INDEX

INDEX

INDEX

IMAGE CREDITS